# EXCHANGES: LIFE AFTER DANCE

# EXCHANGES: LIFE AFTER DANCE

*JOYSANNE SIDIMUS*

Press of Terpsichore

PRESS OF TERPSICHORE LIMITED
TORONTO
1987

## Canadian Cataloguing in Publication Data

Sidimus, Joysanne.
  Exchanges : life after dance

ISBN 0-920251-01-3

1. Ballet dancers - Canada - Biography.  2. Ballet
dancers - United States - Biography.  3. Ballet
dancing.  4. Career changes.  I. Title.

GV1785.A1S54 1987    792.8'2'0922    C87-093299-3

©JOYSANNE SIDIMUS, 1983
ISBN 0-920251-01-3
First printing, 1987

Editor for Press of Terpsichore Limited: Robert S. Williams
Cover Design: John Selleck
Computer Technician: Alison T. McMahon
Typesetting: Jaytype Inc.
Design Consultant: John White
Production: Coach House Press

Press of Terpsichore Limited
P.O. Box 563,
Postal Station Q
Toronto, Ontario
Canada
M4T 2N4

*In memory of*

*ERIK BRUHN*

*whose support and understanding of the problems of transition were integral, both to the writing of this book and to the founding of the Dancer Transition Centre.*

# Contents

Acknowledgments . . . . . . . . . . . . . . . . . . . . . . . . . . . . . . . . . IX

Foreword . . . . . . . . . . . . . . . . . . . . . . . . . . . . . . . . . . . . . . . . XI

Introduction . . . . . . . . . . . . . . . . . . . . . . . . . . . . . . . . . . . . . XIII

Points of View . . . . . . . . . . . . . . . . . . . . . . . . . . . . . . . . . . .  1

### The Artistic Directorship

Erik Bruhn . . . . . . . . . . . . . . . . . . . . . . . . . . . . . . . . . . . . . .  5
Ludmilla Chiriaeff . . . . . . . . . . . . . . . . . . . . . . . . . . . . . . . . .  7
Rosemary Dunleavy . . . . . . . . . . . . . . . . . . . . . . . . . . . . . . . .  9
Richard Englund . . . . . . . . . . . . . . . . . . . . . . . . . . . . . . . . . . 11
Celia Franca . . . . . . . . . . . . . . . . . . . . . . . . . . . . . . . . . . . . . 13
Robert Joffrey . . . . . . . . . . . . . . . . . . . . . . . . . . . . . . . . . . . . 15
Betty Oliphant . . . . . . . . . . . . . . . . . . . . . . . . . . . . . . . . . . . 17
Brydon Paige . . . . . . . . . . . . . . . . . . . . . . . . . . . . . . . . . . . . 19
Arnold Spohr . . . . . . . . . . . . . . . . . . . . . . . . . . . . . . . . . . . . 21
Linda Stearns . . . . . . . . . . . . . . . . . . . . . . . . . . . . . . . . . . . . 23

### The Dancers

Lawrence and Miriam Adams . . . . . . . . . . . . . . . . . . . . . . . 27
Kathleen Bannon . . . . . . . . . . . . . . . . . . . . . . . . . . . . . . . . . 39
James Brusock . . . . . . . . . . . . . . . . . . . . . . . . . . . . . . . . . . . 47
Carolyn George D'Amboise . . . . . . . . . . . . . . . . . . . . . . . . . 55
Christopher Darling . . . . . . . . . . . . . . . . . . . . . . . . . . . . . . . 65
Marian Horosko . . . . . . . . . . . . . . . . . . . . . . . . . . . . . . . . . . 75
Charles Kirby . . . . . . . . . . . . . . . . . . . . . . . . . . . . . . . . . . . . 85
Judith Kupersmith . . . . . . . . . . . . . . . . . . . . . . . . . . . . . . . . 93
Angela Leigh . . . . . . . . . . . . . . . . . . . . . . . . . . . . . . . . . . . . 105
Sam Moses . . . . . . . . . . . . . . . . . . . . . . . . . . . . . . . . . . . . . 117
Andrew Oxenham . . . . . . . . . . . . . . . . . . . . . . . . . . . . . . . . 125
Marcos Paredes . . . . . . . . . . . . . . . . . . . . . . . . . . . . . . . . . . 133
Wendy Reiser . . . . . . . . . . . . . . . . . . . . . . . . . . . . . . . . . . . 143
Nancy Reynolds . . . . . . . . . . . . . . . . . . . . . . . . . . . . . . . . . 153
James Ronaldson . . . . . . . . . . . . . . . . . . . . . . . . . . . . . . . . . 165
Ellen Shire . . . . . . . . . . . . . . . . . . . . . . . . . . . . . . . . . . . . . 173

Arlene Shuler ........................................... 183
Roland Vazquez ........................................ 193
William Weslow ....................................... 201
Valerie Wilder ......................................... 209

# Conclusion ....................................... 221

# acknowledgments

Four years is a long time to work on a book of this length and many people have been invaluable in bringing it to print. When the interviews began, it became quickly apparent that the commitment, joie de vivre, and generosity of spirit that characterized these dancers had not diminished when their performing lives were over. They had danced in an era when bodies were not so perfect and technique not so advanced but passion, drama, and artistry (not to mention entertainment) were vital. Dance, as a profession, was an oddity; not quite respectable. Now, it is fashionable. Neither situation makes it integral to society.

The dancers were interviewed on tape and then given their chapters to review. Many simply re-wrote them; most suggested changes. What emerged is as much their work as mine and, for that and their generosity, I am deeply grateful.

Obviously, the artistic direction of companies has a direct and powerful effect on young dancers' visions of themselves and their ability to look beyond the performer's life. The directors who agreed to be interviewed were also most concerned and articulate on the issue. Many had fought for survival and now were grateful that a time had come when the human element could be discussed. Most had tried within their companies to do what they could, but resources were scarce. Some who were asked to contribute to the book ignored the letters of request; some wanted to but were genuinely too busy; the battle has just begun.

On the practical side, thanks to Elizabeth Long for her work in the early stages of editing. The patience and sensitivity of editor Nenagh Leigh, was extraordinary and I am deeply grateful to her. Thanks, also, to Lally McMahon who typed, re-typed, and remained enthusiastic throughout it all. To the Dance in Canada Association and its Executive Director, Steve Dymond, heartfelt thanks for the use of their computer. Nancy Reynolds, an old friend and fine author, not only agreed to be part of the book but generously gave professional and practical advice. To Assis Carreiro, archivist of the National Ballet of Canada, for her patience and generosity. To Bob Williams, the publisher — a debt of gratitude. When he first heard about the book in a casual conversation at York University, he offered to publish it because he believed it was time the issue was raised in print.

Undaunted by opinions that "it won't sell — it should be a series of magazine articles," he has proceeded to be as caring and meticulous with the material as the dancers. He is an idealist in a world of pragmatists — and a dear friend.

Finally a few personal thanks — to my late mother, Bessie B. Sidimus, and to the late George Balanchine for teaching me to risk and to my husband, John, for his artistry and taste and to my daughter, Anya, who brings joy.

*Joysanne Sidimus*
*Toronto*
*December 11, 1986*

I am so pleased to write the Foreword to this book by Joysanne Sidimus. It can be a tremendously emotional moment for dancers when they realize the time has come to pursue another career. Sometimes it occurs suddenly — as in the case of injury — while at other times a gradual realization that one's dancing days are numbered takes hold. Dancers often have a feeling of inadequacy when faced with the thought of beginning a second career. There is no need for them to feel this way, since the reality is that they are not uneducated or incapable of doing something new and different. Sadly however, many feel this way.

Dancers have been trained to use their powers of observation, their memories, and their feeling for design to a far greater degree than that given by an ordinary education. Since they have known all their lives what they wanted to do and have worked at it with dedication and discipline, each day is approached with an expectation of achievement. It should be stressed that the maturity and security they have attained through dancing will sustain them when the time comes to contemplate another career.

It is worth noticing that many doctors are just completing their training at an age when dancers are ending their careers. A dancer has the advantage, when beginning a second one, of the confidence and the sense of accomplishment that comes from having successfully pursued a dance career. To reinforce their confidence and to ensure they value what they have accomplished, I have worked with Dean Grace Geibel and Professor Jeanne Pearlmann of Carlow College to advise my dancers of the Pittsburgh Ballet Theatre about courses they may take while still performing, which may enhance their lives and prepare them for a career change.

With members of the company we have discussed such issues as the value of work (and peers) as educational vehicles and the importance of avocations in determining future careers. We have identified a group of eight dancers for a first course, for which they will receive college credit. The instructor will come to our building two evenings a week during rehearsal periods until the dancers complete the necessary hours of work. The Carlow curriculum is based on the liberal arts, with significant emphasis on career preparation. The initial course will be a broad study program including the arts and philosophy and has the potential to develop awareness and lead to further possibilities.

I commend this book as a most worthwhile contribution to dance literature, and in particular for the encouragement it can give to dancers who face transition from one career to another.

*Patricia Wilde*
*Artistic Director*
*Pittsburgh Ballet Theatre*

*"I will probably try to make a clean break from this profession because I am very passionately and emotionally tied to dance, and when I can no longer dance professionally it would hurt too much to be reminded of the past."*

*"Time is an important factor — time to think and re-think without panic or financial worry."*

*"I have never seriously thought about stopping dancing. How can you know what you will feel?"*

*"... always having felt myself to be a 'company' person, I would have a difficult time slotting myself into a regular job under someone else ... strange ...."*

*"Being on stage is the safest place in the world ... it's solitary, demanding ... there is no recourse but to commit fully. Knowing that and not having that outlet of expression is painful to contemplate. It's coming and it's not going to be easy."*

The above are quotes from Canadian dancers who were asked to comment on their perceptions of their transition from professional dancing. This book deals with dancers — all of whom have performed with major companies who have made the transition successfully. In addition, they have chosen to make their second careers outside the dance world. The methods and reasons for their choices are as diverse as the professions themselves. In some cases, the devotion and discipline the dance world demanded had become such an integral part of the dancer's life that it was necessary to find a career with much the same demands. For others, the reverse was true; a slower, calmer lifestyle was sought, one that would bring relief from the constant stress and tension. The common element was the communal structure in which they all trained and danced. The careers chosen by the people interviewed indicated a desire for independence. The individuality previously expressed in dance required not only a new career but a lifestyle the ex-dancer could totally control.

The problems faced by retiring performers are many. For most dancers the support structure known from childhood disappears at the same time as the dancing itself, although the joy of movement may remain long after the body can no longer execute the steps. The poignancy of it is that every dancer has been trained to be acutely aware not only of his or her body, but of the realities of dedication, sacrifice, and structure; no one knows better than the dancer when it is not there.

The intention in writing this book was to explore the minds of those whose transition has been other than to the assumed professions of teacher, ballet master, or choreographer (although they too require enormous adjustment and re-education, not to mention talent!) to find out how some have rechannelled the seriousness, discipline, and commitment of their dancing selves to other rewarding pursuits, minimizing the confusion and emotional and physical problems so many retiring dancers experience.

The question applies to a much wider population than the dance world. Mid-life career transition is commonplace. The type of change is similar: a need to move on when either the physical element of executing the job becomes impossible or the job itself becomes obsolete. It is the motivation of the dancer that sets him or her apart. The profession is relentless in its demands, scarce in its material rewards, and fiercely defended by all involved in it. As one sociologist puts it, "It is a downwardly mobile profession in an upwardly mobile society." The guarantees are few — you will work harder than most, make less money than most, and will probably have to retire long before you are middle-aged. Why do it at all? The motivation is simple — dancers dance for the love of it. What happens to them when the performing stops? Some — as those interviewed for this book — have made very successful transitions. Many have not. The performing life of a dancer is intense, insecure, and short. The fact of that life coming to an end is rarely faced and even more rarely planned for.

In the past it was not only the dancer who had no plan for the future. The dance world itself led a precarious life. In North America, native companies first came into being in the thirties and forties, and for the next several decades they struggled merely to exist. Dancers, grossly underpaid, worked under conditions which eliminated all but the most dedicated. To some degree the situation has now changed. A few ballet and modern companies — the rebels in the beginning — are now Establishment. Theatrical dance, once considered a European oddity became, if not integral to society, an accepted part of the cultural scene. Seasons were longer, touring conditions improved, and some companies actually had more performances in their home cities than on tour, allowing the dancers the possibility of a more stable lifestyle. Musical theatre also flourished, and choreographers demanded a greater variety of skills than ever before. The "gypsy" —

the multi-faceted show performer — was born. The growth of television and the development of the "industrial" show also gave opportunities to dancers, and, in the United States, the entrance of government funding encouraged the creation of new "regional" companies. As work became more available the number of professional dancers increased.

While salaries — often negotiated through unions — rose, in the area of pre-retirement planning nothing else changed. Pension systems were few and far between, and unemployment insurance became a form of subsidy for the art. Not unaware of the problem, many companies and directors tried to help by recommending ex-dancers as teachers and directors of regional companies, but because of the increased population, the dance profession could only absorb a small percentage of its own back into what for many was the only world they knew. Many dancers, protected for years by the insular life of the dance world, found difficulty coping with reality at a time when their emotional, spiritual, and financial resources were low.

Although no modern dancers were interviewed for this book, their problems are no less acute. The creativity which characterizes the modern dancer helped many in establishing their own companies and schools. Some continued to dance as they performed their own works, but many, worn down by years of insufficient funding, difficult work conditions, and small audiences, began to look elsewhere. Some have made successful second careers, but like their colleagues in the ballet world many are lost.

The interviews began in 1983 and concluded only recently. Finding a common element in the dancers' approach to their transition proved impossible. In the choice of career, however, one fact did emerge — few were working for anyone else. Most had chosen careers that were either entrepreneurial or professional. Passion, creativity, and fulfillment were the demands.

Society has now benefited twice from this remarkable group of individuals — first as dancers and now in their chosen second careers. Most achieved their success alone, with little or no help. For many the love of dance still pervades their lives, and in their new professions many have made a significant contribution to their art. We are all in their debt.

# POINTS OF VIEW

# THE ARTISTIC DIRECTORSHIP

## *ERIK BRUHN* (1928-1986), Artistic Director, National Ballet of Canada; Formerly Artistic Director, Royal Swedish Ballet

"The career transition of dancers is only now beginning to surface as a serious issue in the dance world. The problem is quite different in Europe because of the pension system, and it has been suggested that something similar to that should exist here. My experience has been that while a pension provides financial security, in some cases it also encourages a retirement of inactivity. While still dancing, there are always a few who will keep a passion for their art alive, but the majority know the comfortable future the pension gives, and the general atmosphere in the company is adversely affected. I would not say that it makes for an artistically burning situation! On the other hand, without pensions, dancers face a sense of urgency about finding a second career at the very time when they need a respite from the pressures of the performer's life. I've come to believe there is no ideal set-up.

I feel one of the solutions to the question is in looking at the problem at a much younger age, while the dancer is still in school. The student must be made aware of the brief life span of the performer and understand that any exploration of other interests can only enhance both the dancing and life after performing. The theatre life should be perceived in a much broader way. This kind of plan works best where both the academic and ballet schools are under one roof, such as at our National Ballet School here in Toronto. However, I believe it's the responsibility of all professional schools to work toward an awareness of the problem.

Once the dancer is with a professional company, I feel that the director has a critical role to play in encouraging the dancer to develop a range of skills. The director should appeal to the dancer to participate in artistic capacities beyond performing. As well, I feel it is the director's responsibility to deal honestly with a dancer who has been with a company for seven or eight years and is in his or her mid-twenties. Any director would know by that time if the dancer has the potential to be a soloist. If they do not, they should be told and, in this way, can leave voluntarily or begin to plan for their future.

Basically, a natural curiosity is one's best asset for a life after dance.

5

I believe the arts are best served by a wide perspective of understanding. If dancers can broaden their mental horizons, I think they will have a greater awareness of their standards and qualities and how to hold on to them. I encourage them to think independently, but in the communal structure this is often very difficult."

## *LUDMILLA CHIRIAEFF,* Founding Artistic Director, Les Grands Ballets Canadiens; Founder and Director, École Supérieure de Danse du Québec

"To live is to be in constant movement and transformation as well. Life, therefore, is MOVEMENT and movement throughout the ages became dance!

For a true servant of the dance, life *after* dance remains movement. A true servant continues, through his transformation, to devote his life to dance in every way possible.

To support a dancer in this process is helping to create life after dance within the dance!"

## *ROSEMARY DUNLEAVY,* Ballet Mistress, New York City Ballet

"As a ballet mistress I can see signs of dancers coming to the end of their career from a technical point of view. I try to talk to them if they are not being cast in ballets they have previously done. If it's somebody who has been in the company for a while, I will approach them and explain why. This is only fair to them and generally leads into a talk about their standing in the company, or about what is happening to them. Each case is highly individual so you can't say exactly what will happen. About three or four years ago we had quite a group preparing to leave; some went to school and some got married.

I think it's a rather healthy situation. People are facing reality more now than they ever were. Unfortunately, however, some are staying only because they realize that it's a good career. The arts have become big business and life in our company is very secure. On the other hand, we have a lot of dancers who are very, very dedicated and love doing it and possibly can love it more because they are more comfortable in their lives. I think the biggest problem of transition is the same problem that has been there for years: dancers admitting to themselves that it's happening. Even if you're told the end of your performing is approaching, it's the dancers' responsibility to admit to themselves that this is really true. It's not anyone's fault; it's not even their fault. It's just a progression."

# RICHARD ENGLUND, Artistic Director, The Joffrey II Dancers; Formerly Artistic Director, American Ballet Theatre II

"I would like to see training, in the conservatory sense, that prepares dancers not only for their dance careers but to be functioning adults and artists. In many cases, because of the pressures of scholarship and training, we remove our dance students from their family environments too early. This may result in a loss of personal completeness that shows up in performance and makes it even more difficult when the moment has come to make a transition.

I would love to see a time when our companies question whether they want dancers at much before the age of twenty. Now our cut-off rate for losing many dancers is middle to late twenties, when emotional and human resources are only starting to be attained. This is, after all, an art and to be an art implies that you are reflecting human conditions and communicating something. I feel this is one of the reasons that once dancers have finished their youthful period of energetic dancing, they wonder what more there is.

In a company, I believe it is the leadership — the kind of vision, the kind of behavior, the daily contact — in short, the way one functions as a director that makes the difference. In America, we have lost virtually all of our founding directors. Those founding directors were a great inspiration. Many of us were very privileged to have been around those people. We now have directors who have a different kind of relationship to their company, their repertory, and their audiences. However, the new directors have to find ways to equally inspire and lead the dancers. It is a very difficult transition period for directors as well as for dancers — a 'coming of age' in an institutionalized field of dance."

11

# CELIA FRANCA, Founder, National Ballet of Canada

"In the early years of the National Ballet of Canada, when perform-ance opportunities were scarce, dancers were so caught up in the challenge and actual act of performing that concerns for the future did not enter their thoughts. Influenced by a dearth of comparable occupations and a lack of preparation for possible alternatives, when finally faced with the fact that their performing careers were over, many members of the dance population arbitrarily made the choice to teach. This was not always wise as the talented dancer is not necessarily a gifted teacher (Margot Fonteyn and other well-known dancers seldom teach). Further, former dancers often feel they have not achieved their potential as performers and the transferral of their frustration to the students exists as a real threat.

As the dance world grew, the problems connected with transition grew as well, and not all the retiring dancers could find employment in existing companies and schools. The dilemma is how to prepare the dancers for the inevitable. I believe this preparation must begin while dancers are still in school. Dance students should not only be made aware of the inevitability of career change (the average dancer's physique will not function adequately after the age of forty), but be provided with the basis for an eventual new career.

Another problem — still unresolved — is that of the artist's right to material benefits similar to those enjoyed by other members of the work force. If, in order to achieve and protect those rights, the artist becomes hard-boiled and loses vulnerability and sensitivity — attrib-utes so essential to the performing artist — the problem is com-pounded. On the other hand, if one is too sensitive and vulnerable, basic rights may be denied. I think it is important that the artist find that delicate balance; that rights be acquired but never at the expense of what is integral and necessary to one's artistic honesty."

# *ROBERT JOFFREY,* Artistic Director, The Joffrey Ballet

"I would encourage my dancers to remain in their own field. Only people who have danced can carry on the traditions of the art. Why should you take twenty years of experience and not utilize it in some way?

It is true, however, that some retired dancers go into teaching without the proper motivation and because they do not know that other options exist. And that is sad because then one will not be a dedicated teacher, one who inspires and enlightens one's pupils.

I can think of so many related careers for dancers. For example, I think the field of dance criticism has suffered because most dance critics have very limited dance backgrounds. However, a writer who has danced can write with great understanding of the quality of movement. In addition to criticism, there is dance notation, stage management, teaching, rehearsing and coaching, arts administration, and dance-related jobs in government agencies, foundations, and corporations. I always say to dancers, 'You have spent most of your life investing in your art, and your experience and understanding will be of value in the market-place. If you are unhappy, then don't do it. However, if you like dance and want to be a part of it, you can give something back to the art.'

Sometimes, in order to have time to heal, it is necessary to go through what I call the scar-tissue period. You stop dancing and you need to take some time to re-evaluate your life and commitments. Sometimes it takes years, during which time you do not want to be involved with dance. Then you realize how much dance really means to you, and you can get on with your life."

## BETTY OLIPHANT, Artistic Director and Ballet Principal, National Ballet School, Toronto

"One of the greatest problems dancers have in their education is that they are not encouraged to develop as mature people. This is partly the result of having to start professional training at an early age when the body is still malleable. Also, because the body is the instrument, the training has to be closely supervised on a daily basis in order to avoid developing bad habits. This close supervision continues even when a dancer becomes professional. Therefore, unless their teachers and coaches help them when they are young to be responsible for themselves, it is difficult for them to mature and develop a sense of artistic independence. At the National Ballet School we encourage our students to think independently. Under the supervision of a fine academic faculty they receive a first-class education. At my school in England there was very little emphasis on related arts such as the history of art, music, drama, etc. I have felt this lack deeply so have tried to provide our students with an enriched curriculum specifically emphasizing the interrelationship of the arts. As well, in order to expose our students to people from all walks of life, we frequently invite guests such as Rostropovitch, Sir Edmund Hillary, David Suzuki, and Yehudi Menuhin to meet with them.

We also emphasize the importance of being sensitive to the students' emotional growth, which is often neglected in this time-consuming profession. To this end, we have a full-time counsellor and a team of psychiatrists to help the students with their strong sense of commitment to their art and the perfectionism which accompanies it.

Dancers have many fine qualities. They are self-disciplined, hard-working, and have the ability to do something in depth. Most, also, relate well to people. With proper education and guidance, they should find fulfillment in whatever career they pursue."

# *BRYDON PAIGE,* Artistic Director, The Alberta Ballet

"It is extremely important that dancers consider their future early in their careers. I was fortunate to have been dancing at a time and place (Montreal in the fifties and sixties), where there were many opportunities to study and perform a wide range of dance forms, providing a rich background invaluable to me as a teacher and choreographer. In addition, while performing with Les Grands Ballets Canadiens, Brian Macdonald and Ludmilla Chiriaeff encouraged me to try my hand at teaching and choreographing.

I have too often seen performers suddenly come to the end of their careers and expect to become teachers, coaches, and choreographers overnight. It takes years to develop one's craft in any of these areas, and if interested, one should try to make use of opportunities to teach and choreograph whenever possible. One of the drawbacks of a career in dance is that it consumes so much time and energy that there is often little left over for pursuing other interests. As performers, we are inclined to totally immerse ourselves in developing technique.

Not everyone is destined to teach and choreograph. It is therefore important to think about alternatives and to take steps to develop other interests in preparation for a new career, and it is particularly important to communicate and relate to people outside of the dance world. Such contacts can be vital in helping to identify and develop a second career."

# *ARNOLD SPOHR,* Artistic Director, Royal Winnipeg Ballet

"It has been my policy to encourage our dancers to express their individuality and be responsible for themselves in the company. In the early days of our company, dancers had to find ways other than dancing to support themselves while being involved in dance. While conditions are different now, I think the question of responsibility remains the same.

A dance company is an important part of the community. It is vital that the dancers and artistic staff meet and associate with the general public, since the public is a valued necessity. Contact between dance artists and the public establishes a rapport and greater understanding is achieved. In this way the dancers also remain part of the real world and can expand their knowledge of it.

Dancers need to be responsible for their own minds and bodies. Intelligence is very important for dancers since they need to be self-sufficient concerning their future. It's important for dancers to contribute back into their own profession, and in our company, after an eight to nine year performing cycle, a dancer can move into teaching, choreography, administration or other areas, in either the company or the school. Continuity in the profession is essential.

The role of the artistic director is to strongly lead the whole ballet company. He or she guides, nurtures, and makes final decisions in all matters. The artistic director has the responsibility of guiding his artists in their careers, and of seeking out their talents and achieving growth. He or she must help them in ways not only associated with dance, but by broadening and increasing their skills in preparation for the future. There should be time for them to develop interests and contacts in the outside world. Our five-day work week was established to support this. We have open company meetings during the year if necessary, at which dancers and other company members can bring up issues and get input about our policies.

With personal guidance from within the company and from outside organizations and contacts, dancers can find their own way in a transition from performing to another career. I think that in the future more dancers will come back to dance in some way because it is natural for them — it was their initial impulse.

The dancer should be made aware that there is life after dance.

Encouragement should be given by the artistic director to a dancer showing talent in other areas of the dance profession. A dancer could move into teaching, choreography, stage management, or administration. The artistic director of the future should come from the dancers of today. Dancers fully realize and totally understand what dance and dancers are all about, and you would then have an intelligent, knowledgeable, dance-oriented staff. If not interested in or capable of these responsibilities, the dancer needs to be motivated to seek a job outside of dance. Everything is relative."

# *LINDA STEARNS,* Co-Artistic Director, Les Grands Ballets Canadiens

"Transition from performing came sooner for me than I had anticipated — before I felt ready to stop dancing. I was fortunate that Les
Grands Ballets Canadiens had a tradition of helping their own artists
resituate their careers within its own organization. Madame Chiriaeff, then the Artistic Director when I was dancing with the company, had a theory about dancer transition. She believed in trying to
absorb dancers back into company life, and had the knack of sensing
just exactly where, within the company structure, a particular dancer
might possibly fit. I had particularly wanted to stay within the theatre
atmosphere of dance and at that time the company needed additional
help. They saw potential in me and I started training as an assistant to
Fernand Nault (Co-Artistic Director) towards a career as a ballet
mistress.

My teacher, Bettina Byers, was the first to help me see that theatre
life was not easy, and she taught me how to cope. M. Nault's superb
coaching and guidance brought me to my new métier with care and
compassion. In the years following Mme. Chiriaeff and M. Nault as its
directors, Les Grands Ballets Canadiens has continued to practice this
policy wherever applicable to a dancer. We have several members of
our staff who quite happily have made the transition to administrative
positions within the company.

I like this method myself. There is an inner rhythm in a dance
company which ex-dancers know about. I find that they are far more
adept at adjusting to administering the planning of company schedules, touring demands, union rules, theatre requirements, and other
situations within company life than perhaps someone with experience in an outside field. Outsiders tend to have more difficulty
adjusting to that particular rhythm. I also think that it can be especially important for the men of the company, who perhaps carry a
greater financial responsibility in life, that they be absorbed back into
the company structure, if there is the potential talent and capability.

I do have enormous respect for most of our dancers who take
advantage of the opportunities that touring affords them and who
find time to go to concerts, art galleries, museums, and libraries,
broadening their education and enlarging their life experience which
is imperative to their later careers, whatever they may choose.

While our company has improved the working conditions for the dancer and strives continually to refine these conditions, my main concern is that the dancer's transition will be treated with care, positive encouragement, and humanity."

# THE DANCERS

# LAWRENCE AND
# MIRIAM ADAMS

*"If there were something called 'Art,' I thought that somehow dancing should be a part of that, or be useful for that or be an aspect of that."*

Lawrence Adams

*"After you've been a flower and a snowflake for seven years, and there doesn't look like there's going to be anything else to do, you become disenchanted."*

Miriam Adams

*Photograph by Ken Bell*

Photograph by Ken Bell

*Photograph by Cylla von Tiedemann with permission from Miriam Adams*

# LAWRENCE ADAMS

*Lawrence began his ballet training in Toronto at several summer programs offered by the National Ballet School. He subsequently joined the National Ballet of Canada in 1954. Early in his career he stopped dancing for a year. He returned to dance, first with Les Grands Ballets Canadiens and then with the Joffrey Ballet, before rejoining the National Ballet of Canada as a soloist and later a principal dancer. He left the National Ballet in 1969.*

# MIRIAM ADAMS

*Miriam began her ballet training with Betty Oliphant in Toronto and continued at the National Ballet School. Upon graduating she joined the National Ballet of Canada and danced with them for seven years, during which time she met Lawrence Adams. Lawrence and Miriam were married in 1967 and left the company in 1969.*

*Since leaving the company, the pair have operated an antique shop and an art gallery, pioneered Canada's first experimental dance space, founded and published two dance news publications, a homebuilt aircraft magazine, and a video magazine, and have produced their own programming for cable television. They are now working on* Encore! Encore! — *a project to preserve Canadian theatrical dance history and create a living museum available through a national data-base network. Miriam is also a board member of the Dancer Transition Centre and the Toronto Arts Council.*

*Miriam:* When Betty Oliphant first came to Toronto, my mother took me to study with her. At first she taught in a church, and I continued studying with her both in her studio on Sherbourne Street and at the National Ballet School.

I was sixteen when the school opened, and I was encouraged to go because I was told I'd have a far better chance at being a professional dancer and of getting into the National Ballet of Canada if I went to the school. At first I said no, because I was having too much fun at high school and had my own group of friends. For a while I stayed in a regular high school but was again told that if I really wanted to do ballet I had to go to the National Ballet School. By this time I seemed to have the physical capability and talent for it. So I said, "All right," got my uniform, and went to the school for Grades 11 and 12 and one year of post-graduate work.

Eventually, I did join the company, but I always felt outside of it somehow. We would sit in the dressing room before a performance and everybody would be putting on their makeup, and I would look

31

around and think "What the hell am I doing? I don't really feel right doing this." Mind you, I did it for seven years. I felt that was where I was for that period of time, but it wasn't a passion in my life. At the same time, I felt there was something important there.

Everybody told me it looked easy for me, but I couldn't stand on my toes very well and mentally it was difficult because I didn't have any confidence in myself. On the other hand, I didn't have any sort of futuristic vision of anything else. I was there while I was there, but it wasn't comfortable. I often felt silly being a gingerbread, a flower, and a snowflake.

*Lawrence:* I guess I've never really thought about this. I don't know if I was passionate about it or not. I always felt that somewhere in dancing there was a tremendous value. I don't know whether it was for me or for the audience. I guess I lived under the illusion that the depth was there, somewhere.

I come from Winnipeg. My brother, David Adams, was a dancer, and I used to go and see performances of the Royal Winnipeg Ballet when I was a little kid. One day I decided I wanted to go to Toronto. I was fifteen and the National Ballet had a summer school, and I wanted to go and dance. There was one male to forty females, so every time a male walked in the door everybody got all excited.

I learned a great deal in those six weeks. Then I went back to Winnipeg and hung around for a year, and came back to Toronto for the following two summers. Shortly after the third summer, I joined the National Ballet. I think my starting salary was something like thirty-five dollars a week and that's what almost everybody was being paid. There was a lot of poverty. After five years with the company I stopped dancing for a year because I didn't think I wanted to dance. I did all kinds of things. I used to build furniture and I got into electronics. I was fortunate when I'd been in grade school to have had a carpentry teacher who taught me woodworking skills.

I was fortunate in ballet too, because I had the kind of body which didn't give me too much trouble after a year off. You lose the ability, but keep the technique! Nevertheless, after that year, the National wouldn't take me back. I suppose it was because I was outspoken. I didn't think that what the company was doing was particularly challenging. If there were something called "Art," I thought that somehow dancing should be a part of that, or be useful for that or be an aspect of that. In any event, I was accepted by Les Grands Ballets Canadiens but I found little challenge there as well.

Then, on a lay-off, I was doing a musical in Seattle and Gerald Arpino was there. He saw me dance and asked me to audition for the Joffrey company. I did, and I then joined that company.

I found that the Joffrey company was like working inside a stainless steel cage. It was my first exposure to U.S. dance, and there's no question that the dancers that were in the company at that time were good. They were physically great. They had six male dancers who were fantastic, but that whole sort of perfection thing bored me. I had never rehearsed so much in my life! Technique is okay up to a point, but after a while it becomes boring. I couldn't have cared less.

I came back to Toronto in the summer, and I went to meet Celia Franca. We made a deal and that was that. I re-joined the National Ballet.

*Miriam:* That was the year I joined the company.

*Lawrence:* Life in the company was pretty easy at that point because I was old enough and had been through enough to know how to cope. I was a soloist and became a principal; I began to be respected and had much more room to grow.

*Miriam:* Not me! I didn't have anything interesting or challenging to do. I was with twenty-four other girls, and I had to be the same as everyone else. It was hard because I felt uncomfortable with it. I did take a creative writing correspondence course in my last couple of years there, but, other than that, I didn't do anything else.

*Lawrence:* There was time to do other things if you wanted to. Yves Cousineau and I set up a workshop on the third floor in the back of the St. Lawrence Hall, and we started buying junk. We finally decided that we had so much junk we'd better start doing something about it. So we opened an antique shop — "Adams & Yves." We had it about seven years.

*Miriam:* About that time — 1967 — Lawrence and I got married — our Centennial Project — and we left the company in the summer of 1969. In my case, after you've been a flower and a snowflake for seven years, and there doesn't look like there's going to be anything else to do, you become disenchanted.

33

*Lawrence:* I had a lot of fun with the company. I really did. But for me, performing was not that interesting as an investigative process, and I think one of the things that I've discovered in being involved in the arts is that the arts basically operate and come alive because of some investigation. We never did that as dancers, and I think most dancers don't.

*Miriam:* The transition was easy for us because at that time we had the antique shop and we had opened an art gallery. That came about because we had some prints of designs for National Ballet costumes. It seemed that this was a place and time for Canadian artists to show their work. It wasn't practical though; we lost our shirts on that! Then, I was fortunate to be offered a job as administrator for the Nightengale Art Gallery. I took the job and met many visual artists, which gave me a new perspective.

We taught for Lois Smith during this time as well. Some of our students expressed an interest in choreography. We decided to rent a theatre, encourage them to do some choreography, and do some ourselves. When we did our first show, everyone had to take responsibility for things other than dancing or choreographing. We had to learn lighting, how to make tapes, costumes, do publicity, etc. It was a great success and we had a wonderful time.

*Lawrence:* We decided to do more of that. I felt there were a lot of things that could be done. We made mistakes, but we learned really fast. There were fifteen dancers to start with, and we ended up with only five or six when we moved our gallery business into a warehouse.

*Miriam:* We had a thirty-by-forty-foot space there and actually built a little theatre. Lawrence instructed us on how to make a dimmer board, hang lights, run the cables, and put down a floor. We built a theatre from scratch.

*Lawrence:* What we had was a theatre with forty-one seats in the round. It was a fantastic little place. Very, very sensitive. It was an amazing space to be in and to perform in, because the farthest you could get away from anybody was twenty-five feet, and even then you were only two feet away from somebody else. Everything showed. There were all kinds of incredible events happening in what was then a new dance performance environment. We called it "15 Dance Lab" because we had fifteen dollars in the bank when it opened. What we did, eventually, was to provide Canada with its first experimental dance space, and over the years one hundred choreographers passed through its doors!

*Miriam:* We were very adventurous. We bought a small printing press for ten dollars, and we designed our own programs and publicity in an attempt to change the images associated with dance.

*Lawrence:* There were only three rules: don't open the back door, don't wrap the wires around the pipes, and don't smoke dope. Otherwise, do what you want. The artists were responsible from beginning to end.

*Miriam:* We were funded by the Ontario Arts Council, who were very sympathetic to our new ideas.

*Lawrence:* We couldn't have done it otherwise.

*Miriam:* Grant Strate had started a dance department at York University and the graduates were articulate, inventive, and daring. They questioned. Many dancers and choreographers from that group came to 15 Dance Lab to try things out. The performances were not what everybody was used to as far as dance was concerned. Those were really interesting people and they did some incredible work.

*Lawrence:* We finally closed it in 1980. The whole thing was an experiment and its time had come. We wanted anyone coming in the door to walk out a different person. The place itself forced you to deal with everything you did in a totally unique way. But as it went along, it started to become an inexpensive place to do your dancing. It became a poor man's theatre. Most of all, it got quite predictable.

People had started to use galleries and places like that for performances. We felt we had done whatever we had set out to do. These things are finite. It wasn't intended to be an institution. So we stopped.

*Miriam:* We wanted to take dance past the performance experience. We wanted people to think about it, write about it, describe what they were doing, and review what their friends were doing. We had started a small newspaper called *Spill* (published 1976-1978), where we encouraged dancers to write and to look at what other people were doing. It was at that time, I guess, an "underground" publication. It became relatively political. We questioned a lot of funding sources and what was going on in the rest of the country. We were connected with a gallery in Toronto called "A Space," which was doing a lot of avant-garde work, and we had access to the printing facilities there. They had a big press and cameras, and we used these to put together the newspaper, *Spill*. We printed and designed it ourselves. It lasted for thirteen issues.

We placed it in stores and distributed it through the mail. There were several hundred subscribers, but in fact, by number thirteen, there were not enough people reading it. It was costing us money and we had to stop.

*Lawrence:* Around this time I got interested in flying, and flying is expensive. I found out that there were people who built their own airplanes, and I started building one. Then I found out that there was no information in Canada about homebuilt aircraft. So I said, "What we need is a publication." I started a little publication and one thing led to another and I ended up publishing a glossy magazine.

*Miriam:* We also used the theatre as a video facility, as we had acquired some video equipment, and we began to publish a video magazine. So we had, in fact, three publications going: *Spill, Canadian Home-Built Aircraft* and *Video Magazine*. Then we decided that what we needed was a typesetting machine and a computer, so that we could take on job work and do our own publishing. We started a typesetting business. We did programs, flyers, posters, and small arts newspapers for other organizations, and that's how we were able to produce our own publications cheaply. It enabled us to start *Canadian Dance News* as well. This publication covered all the dance activity in Canada, from the National Ballet to the newest independent choreographer, and they both got equal space on the front page.

One of the reasons for starting *Canadian Dance News* was that there's a lot more going on in dance in Canada than anybody imagines. We funded it through ads, but in 1982 there was a recession and the dance community couldn't afford the advertising. Because of that, we had to stop.

One of our two projects now is the Arts Television Centre, an open access facility for the arts community. The studio is available to dancers, theatre people, and video artists. It's sort of an extension of 15 Dance Lab. We decided to do our own television productions and be producers of programming for cable television. We did a series on nine Canadian poets and a series called *Information Dance*, and *The Dance Weather Report*, which included artists' interviews and general dance information. We also did a live series called *Nightlights*, which was a Toronto-based arts news report. Now we are working on *Encore! Encore!* — a project to reconstruct choreographies created by Canadian pioneer dance artists and a living museum called *The Dance Collection*.

When I think about all these different things we've done and will probably continue to do, it seems that it's a matter of having learned some survival skills. I knew when I was twelve years old I wanted to be a ballet dancer, and I couldn't relate to anything else. I didn't care about anything else. I think now that one has to be very open-minded and flexible. That's something we found out when we were over thirty, and that's a little late because you've wasted a lot of time.

*Lawrence:* I think the trick is to put people into a situation where they can experience as many things as possible as quickly as possible. I think the era of the specialist is over. We're generalists and it works for us!

# KATHLEEN BANNON

*"I've found that transitions in life are much like dancing: with ninety percent hard work and ten percent luck and talent, you will succeed."*

*Photograph by Maurice Seymour*

*Photograph by Geoff Steele with permission from Kathleen Bannon*

# EXCHANGES: LIFE AFTER DANCE

*Kathleen was born in Washington, D.C., and received her early dance and music training at the College Conservatory of Music in Cincinnati, Ohio. By the age of fifteen, she was dancing professionally and had returned to Washington, D.C. At the Washington School of Ballet, she combined her ballet and high school studies and performed with the Washington Ballet. After graduating from the Washington School of Ballet in 1964, she joined the newly-founded Harkness Ballet of New York and toured internationally with the company for three years.*

*During these tours, Kathleen became increasingly interested in dance management and international cultural exchange. Several mentors encouraged her to pursue a university degree and a career in international arts management, and she entered American University in Washington, D.C., in 1967. Two and a half years later, she graduated Magna Cum Laude with a major in communication (Radio and TV), and extensive experience in teaching and broadcasting.*

*In 1970, she joined the management staff of the Wolf Trap Center for the Performing Arts in Virginia, and was later invited by the National Endowment for the Arts to develop and direct an arts management training program. In 1977 she was named the Endowment's first Director of International Activities, and for nine years she worked with embassies, corporations, and arts organizations to develop international festivals and artist exchanges.*

*In 1986, Kathleen became the Executive Director of International Arts Enterprises, Inc., an international arts organization located in Washington, D.C.*

"I was born in Washington, D.C., and spent my early years in Cincinnati, Ohio, which offered a splendid range of professional arts organizations and activities. My mother enrolled me in ballet, music, theatre, and art classes when I was eight. I found dance the most stimulating and challenging. Looking back, I realize that the discipline and diligence learned in those classes have influenced my entire life.

I studied ballet with Marian LaCour at the College Conservatory of Music. She balanced our technique classes with opportunities to perform and we appeared frequently with the Cincinnati Symphony, the Cincinnati Summer Opera, and various arts festivals. These performances played a major role in teaching us that a performing career demanded discipline and total dedication — quite a valuable lesson at such an early age.

By the time I was thirteen, I had decided to become a dancer. I turned professional at fifteen with a performance at the Cincinnati Summer Opera. That fall, my family moved to Washington, D.C., and I completed the last year of high school at the Washington School of Ballet. The school had a wonderful curriculum which combined academic and dance classes. Our academic classes were very small — three or four students — and were designed to integrate our interest in dance with traditional course work. For example, French classes covered theatre and dance history, while history classes related the performing and visual arts to political and economic events. We had splendid teachers at the Washington School of Ballet, including Anatole Vilzak and Ludmilla Schollar of the Diaghilev Ballet, who gave us a sense of dance history and continuity with the past. Mr. Vilzak's memories of the premiere of *Sacre de Printemps*, graduation performances at the Maryinsky (now the Kirov) Theater, and the blue of the Monte Carlo sky continue to haunt my own memories of life at the ballet school.

One of the most difficult aspects of dance training is the conflict that occurs between academic and dance classes. It's very difficult to balance the demands of a normal high school with ballet rehearsal and class schedules. The Washington School of Ballet offered an ideal solution, because the academic teachers understood that when students were rehearsing for *The Nutcracker* they didn't have time to study for exams. The school also fostered a healthy atmosphere of professional respect, because we were competing with each other on the basis of dance talent as well as academic ability.

I had such fine training at the Washington School of Ballet that I felt prepared to audition for the Harkness Ballet which was then being formed. I had never auditioned professionally before and thought I might learn from the experience. To my surprise I was accepted into the company and began rehearsals before graduating from high school.

Of course, I found company life very different from the school atmosphere. The Harkness Ballet was a strong professional company and the dancers were extremely competitive. I was the youngest member of the company and was a 'very green seventeen.' Fortunately, Mrs. Harkness, Jeannot Cerrone (the General Manager), and several of the dancers played very special roles in encouraging and guiding me. I danced with the Harkness Ballet from 1964 to 1967, during which time we did several international tours.

Mrs. Harkness had a policy of commissioning new choreography, music scores, and set and costume designs for most of the ballets in the repertory. The dancers were exposed to some of the most creative

43

minds in dance and theatre. We also met artists in other disciplines, critics, diplomats, and business officials. It was the most wonderful education one could imagine. On tour I found myself learning important lessons backstage by watching Jeannot Cerrone very carefully. He is a wonderful manager with fifty years of dance experience. I was fascinated by his style of management and by the impact that good management has on a company. On stage, I often looked out at the audience and thought how little I knew about the front of the house, lighting and costume design, and the day-to-day operations of the company. As we traveled, my perspective changed.

On my twentieth birthday, I decided to shift careers from performing into management and cultural exchange. I had long conversations with Mr. Cerrone, Donald Saddler, and others. They were aware that I had been taking college-level correspondence courses on tour and that these were inadequate for my needs. They suggested that I enroll at a university for training in management and international relations.

I left an exciting company that had provided remarkable opportunities and returned to the discipline of school. It was not a difficult transition because I felt certain that I would remain in the arts for the rest of my life and that management would be as creative and satisfying in its way as performing had been. Over the years, I continued to receive encouragement from Jeannot Cerrone and Mrs. Harkness, and my ties with the ballet world and Harkness dancers remained intact. I think it is a mistake to neglect the dance world after you stop dancing. You never really stop being a dancer!

For about six years after leaving the Harkness, I taught dance in several private schools in Washington, D.C. Like many former dancers, I found the transition to a less active state somewhat difficult. While I had no problem adjusting mentally and emotionally, I must admit I had a problem with metabolism. The body goes through a difficult adjustment when you change from eight hours of dancing each day to much less activity.

In 1967, I enrolled at American University in Washington, D.C., and completed my studies in two and a half years. That involved taking six courses each semester, year round. The discipline I had learned in ballet stood me in good stead; I graduated Magna Cum Laude. But looking back, I would like to have taken more time with my studies and really savored the experience. Once you graduate, learning opportunities are different and time to study becomes a luxury.

While I attended the university, I shifted my professional interests to communication and had a number of opportunities to work in radio and television. After graduating, I joined the staff of a nationwide radio and TV program, *Call For Action*. I was interested in having broadcasting experience because I felt TV would soon play an essential role in dance. With technical and managerial experience in broadcasting, I would be prepared to translate dance into a different language with satellite, cable, and network productions.

However, after a year and a half in broadcasting, I wanted to return to the arts and was hired by the Wolf Trap Center for the Performing Arts to teach television production to professional and student dancers — a perfect bridge between two careers. Later, I joined the Center's administrative staff and stayed for two seasons.

In 1972, I visited the National Endowment for the Arts which was then a very young federal agency. By sheer coincidence a friend who was an Endowment Director saw me in a corridor and introduced me to a number of Endowment officials. The interviews felt like a series of auditions, and in the end I was introduced to Nancy Hanks, the Endowment's Chairman. During our conversation she asked, 'Would you know how to develop an arts management training program?' I answered,'Of course!' Actually, I had no idea what an arts management program might involve. But in 1972, arts management was a new concept, and no one knew what it really meant. A week later I was hired to develop the Endowment's training program for arts managers.

The Management Fellowship Program was inaugurated in 1973 and is still in operation. Its long-term effects make it one of the Endowment's most interesting efforts. Since the program began, 500 arts managers have been trained and now form a network of managers in the U.S. and other countries. Developing the program was very much like creating a new piece of choreography. I was given the freedom to experiment with the selection of participants and seminar speakers, to change program directions, and to make mistakes.

In 1977, Livingston Biddle was named by President Carter as the new Endowment Chairman. I had had the opportunity to work with Mr. Biddle in earlier years and could see that the Carter administration, and Mrs. Joan Mondale especially, would generate a new dynamism in the arts. The Endowment was a wonderful place to be in those years. Shortly after he arrived, Mr. Biddle asked me if I would like to be Director of the International Program that he planned to establish. Years before as a dancer, I had hoped to work in international arts exchange. The opportunity had finally come.

I spent the next nine years working with many diplomats, foreign governments, U.S. agencies, arts organizations, artists, corporations, and foundations to develop a series of international festivals, new exchanges, and expanded arts support. I had a wonderful opportunity to see the arts grow and change in this country and abroad, and the satisfaction of playing a part. In this new phase, there were again special people who encouraged me, including Mr. Biddle and David Searles, the agency's Deputy Chairman. In management there are sometimes mentors who play the same role as a choreographer may to a particular dancer — that of nurturing and teaching.

After thirteen years with the National Endowment, I recently decided to make another transition and join several associates in establishing a new international exchange organization, International Arts Enterprises, Inc. Again, I feel well prepared. I've found that transitions in life are much like dancing: with ninety percent hard work and ten percent luck and talent, you will succeed."

# JAMES BRUSOCK

*"What advice would I give to dancers today? Just fight for the real and the true, for what you feel in your heart and what you really want to do. Go ahead and do it, don't listen to anybody else, and have a good time doing it!"*

Photograph by Constantine

Photograph by Delia Peters

*James was born in Detroit, Michigan, and grew up on a small farm outside Detroit. Influenced by the dancing he saw in movies, he began studying tap dancing when he was seven. At age twelve, he saw a performance of the Ballet Russe de Monte Carlo in Detroit and immediately registered for an intensive summer course in ballet. He continued his ballet studies, and at sixteen went to New York where he successfully auditioned for the Ballet Russe. He danced with them for two years, spent a year studying and working in Paris, and then worked for two years in television before joining the New York City Ballet with whom he danced for three years.*

*At twenty-six, after a ten-year career as a dancer, he decided to stop dancing. He first became a hairdresser, working in many top New York salons. He was then invited to create a makeup and hair department at the New York City Ballet. He worked with them for seven years, developing and expanding that department. More recently, James has moved on to freelance makeup work for fashion and beauty magazines.*

"I grew up on a small farm in Livonia, Michigan, outside Detroit where I was born. I discovered dance at a very early age. At two and a half or three, someone set me in the middle of the floor and said, 'Twirl!' I used to love to 'twirl,' and I found that if I danced I easily won attention and money. Relatives would throw money at my feet. The money went into a savings bank and eventually got me to New York.

I started studying tap dancing at seven, mostly because of the movies. When I was twelve, the Ballet Russe de Monte Carlo came to Detroit for their annual season, and I went to see a matinee performance. It was *Swan Lake, Nutcracker* and *Scheherezade*, one of their 'ham and eggs' programs, and I fell in love with it. I immediately registered for a summer course. The teacher was Joey Harris from London, Ontario, who used to partner Mia Slavenska. He thought I was very talented and I convinced my parents, who were against the whole idea, to pay for the courses. Then it became a compulsion, and I threw myself like a horse with blinders into dance study. I quit school when I was sixteen and came to New York with my savings.

In New York, I auditioned for the Ballet Russe and was accepted. I stayed with them for two years, touring all over the United States. Then I did winter stock for Papermill Playhouse and City Center revivals of *Brigadoon* and *The Pajama Game*. I rejoined the Ballet Russe for another year, and then realized I didn't want to stay any longer. I went to Paris for a year to study and try to get work. When I came back, I did a couple of years of television work and toured with Bambi Lynn and Ron Alexander in a small dance company. I then joined the New York City Ballet.

I danced with that company for three years, and during that time I began to realize that I didn't really want to dance. For me, dancing was a way of getting away from the chicken farm, which I hated. Dance is an exotic world and, being an exotic person, had suited me at the time. I enjoyed it very, very much, at first. That's what I wanted to do then, and I tried very hard to do it well and had a wonderful time doing it. It was later on, after I had joined the New York City Ballet, that I thought I was losing interest in performing. I discovered that I just didn't want to do it anymore, in spite of the fact that I enjoyed dancing in Balanchine's ballets.

I'm good at anything I do because I put my whole heart and soul into it. If you want anything in life, you can go and make it happen. I mean, we're all talented! It's just a matter of degree. I didn't want to dance anymore, but I didn't know what I did want to do. I had joined my first ballet company when I was sixteen and had never finished high school. In those days (the sixties), you had to have at least a high school diploma and more often a college degree. I was twenty-six, I had danced for ten years, and I really didn't know what to do.

A friend of mine, Martin Scheepers, who danced with Ballet Theatre, suggested that we go to hairdressing school because he didn't particularly want to dance anymore either. So I said, 'Well, that's a good enough idea.' As a child I'd been very interested in makeup with back yard theatrics, and I'd had to put makeup on for ten years while I was dancing. In fact, I'd always been interested in drawing and painting, so I thought, 'Well, it might be good.' But I really wasn't all that interested in hair, so going to hairdressing school was just a way of making money. I went to school, got my diploma and license, and started working almost immediately in salons here in New York: Lily Daché, Helena Rubenstein, Kenneth's, and the Plaza Hotel.

I found that I didn't like the salon atmosphere. I thought the whole thing was ridiculous and silly. The work wasn't as creative as I'd thought it would be, and it wasn't the kind of work I thought I should be doing or was interested in doing. But it was a way of making a living. Then I just stopped everything for about a year, took a sabbatical, and went and lived in St. Thomas, Virgin Islands. I cut hair to pay my rent and just enjoyed the sun and had a great time. After a while, however, I got bored and needed the sparkle and energy of New York again. So I came back, and just as I did, Eddie Bigelow from the New York City Ballet called and asked if I would be interested in helping them do some wigs for the principals and supers for their production of *Firebird*. I said, 'Sure.' So, I went back and one thing lead to another and it worked out to be a full-time position. They had never had a makeup or hair department before. In fact, no American ballet company had ever had one. It was a first, and I kept the department growing.

I did straight makeup, character makeup, children's, supers', everything from turning Victor Castelli completely grey and silver for *Variations pour une Porte et une Soupir* to creating all the wigs and hairstyles. Basically, anything that happened from the neck up was my department. Mr. Balanchine gave me full rein to do what I wanted and would then either approve it, nix it, or change it. He wanted me to establish a uniform look of beauty throughout the company.

Balanchine was a genius, and it was a great pleasure and a learning experience to work with him. It was a joy just to sit and listen to him with his wealth of experience. He knew so much about so many different things and had rubbed elbows with all the 'greats' of the art and music world. He was more than willing to pass on all he knew to anybody who would listen. I loved it. I was there for seven years, but then, I'm one of those people who has to keep moving on to something new.

Now I've moved into a different area. I met a European freelance makeup artist who was doing fashion and beauty for magazines and advertising, and I thought that freelancing would be a good idea. But I didn't know how to go about doing that. And he said, 'Well, how do you go about anything? You begin.' It's true — you have to start someplace! He gave me a lot of help, including introductions to magazines and to beauty and fashion editors. Getting a portfolio of my work together took a long time. I found that I had to change and soften my approach to makeup. (I had been used to the theatrical situation, with an audience of two to three thousand people.) I still do hair once in a while, but I really don't like doing it.

I like the idea that I'm my own business. I'm a one-man show. I have an agent and it's just like being in the theatre. For now, it's wonderful. I work with many different people, travel a lot, make a hell of a lot more money than I did in the ballet, and have lots of free time. I live minute by minute, and I have no idea who I'm going to be tomorrow.

Who knows? Who cares? There's too much happening right now. Each day for me is like a Persian miniature — there's so much going on and so many people to see. I know some dancers who are not interested in anything but dancing. I think that's leading a very narrow life. I don't understand why people who live in New York don't take advantage of the galleries, museums and theatres. Even if you don't have any money, there are a zillion free events. This is an artistic capital of the world. So take advantage, learn, go and take a free course, prepare!

Dancers often have this notion that something they begin is going to be forever. Nothing need be forever and nothing is forever. It's a false sense of security that people need, and dance companies foster and nurture it to a degree. But company managers know that these dancers aren't going to be there twenty years from now. While they want you to do what they want and they're paying you a salary to do it, it's up to individuals to take responsibility for their own lives. I've always fought for my individuality and independence because I felt instinctively that's how I wanted to live. I was always rebelling in any ballet company I was in when it seemed that they wanted me to do things I didn't believe in. I would do it reluctantly, only because I was there and being paid.

I think society has changed drastically for everybody, and we've all become caught up in it to a certain extent. I've fought against it because I don't like the direction it's been going — towards laziness. People can't walk anymore — they have to take the car to the corner to get a loaf of bread or a quart of milk. I grew up in the country, and I used to have to walk miles to get anyplace. New York is a city to walk in. I've never had a car here. I enjoy renting a car to go out of town for the weekends, but I love to walk and exercise. People are starting to exercise more now — that's one good thing. We've gone through twenty years of sitting. People have become lazy. They've been too well fed and haven't really had to fight for anything. The kids growing up in this atmosphere have had everything given to them. They're given cars when they're sixteen, new clothes all the time, anything they want. Everybody's gotten fat, slothful, and comfortable. They don't even know how to buy broccoli and cook it! They only know how to buy frozen broccoli at twice the price and cook that!

I don't envy kids growing up today. I think it must be very rough. I was fortunate in growing up on a farm where we grew and made everything ourselves. Kids, dancers, young people today, they're all

53

in the same boat. Our way of life is being re-evaluated. I would say go back to the land, eat vegetables and whole grains, and don't eat white bread and junk food. Growing up eating that kind of food for ten or fifteen years, what's it going to do to your brain, much less your body? Recently, there has been a reversal. People are becoming more aware and I find this very hopeful. What advice would I give to dancers today? Just fight for the real and the true, for what you feel in your heart and what you really want to do. Go ahead and do it, don't listen to anybody else, and have a good time doing it! That's really where it's at."

# CAROLYN GEORGE D'AMBOISE

*"I have had such a fortunate and wonderful life and I owe much of it to my training as a dancer. Dancers have discipline and energy. Those two ingredients translate into success in any career. Add to that Mr. Balanchine's often-heard demand, 'Do it today like you are going to die tomorrow,' and you have an unbeatable combination."*

Photograph by Romaine with permission from Carolyn D'Amboise

# CAROLYN GEORGE D'AMBOISE

*Photograph by Carolyn D'Amboise*

*Carolyn began her dance studies in Dallas, Texas. She performed in summer musicals there before traveling to New York City, where she studied at the School of American Ballet. After touring the United States with musical productions, Carolyn joined the San Francisco Ballet, dancing with them for three years. In 1952, she joined the New York City Ballet, where she became a soloist, and danced with the company for four years. During that time she met Jacques D'Amboise, and they were married in 1956. Carolyn left the company for the birth of her first son, George. He was followed by a second son, Christopher, and twin daughters Charlotte and Catherine. Since leaving the ballet and raising their children, Carolyn has launched into a busy and productive career as a photographer but still finds time to teach dance regularly.*

"I remember begging my parents to let me take dancing lessons. When I was seven years old, they finally agreed to let me study with the Kingsbury sisters in Dallas, Texas, my home town. There were ballet classes augmented by acrobatic, tap, and baton twirling. Acrobatics were my favorite because they got more applause at recital time.

By thirteen, dance classes had lost their challenge for me. I didn't realize then that you could change your body with exercise. I thought you were just born with a good technique or not. My energies and free time went for my new love, basketball. We really did have a good team and even won the state championship.

Two years later, on a lark, I auditioned for Dallas summer musicals. A few local dancers were hired to supplement the professional group brought in from New York City for the season. To my surprise I was one of the local dancers chosen. For the next four summers I performed in ten musicals a season. Patricia Bowman appeared in several musicals each summer. Watching her at rehearsals and during performances, I realized how little I knew about ballet technique. It was during those summers that my desire to be a professional dancer took root. The next problem was to get to New York City. My parents were intent on a college education for me. After my first year of college, the choreographer of the summer musicals, Carl Randall, and his wife Fanette told my parents that they should give me the opportunity to study at the Balanchine school. They offered to drive me to New York City and to keep an eye on me there. My parents gave in and let me go, thinking I would be back in Dallas in a month, homesick and miserable, but I loved everything about the city and my teachers at the School of American Ballet.

It was important for me to prove to my parents that it was possible to make a living in the theatre. I made a promise to myself never to ask them for money. After six months in New York my savings from the summer musicals were running out. I auditioned for the musical *Bloomer Girl* and was accepted. After a run at City Center we went on a six-month nationwide tour that closed in California. Next I danced in *Oklahoma!* While performing in San Francisco, I took classes at the San Francisco Ballet School and found the training to be just what I needed. The Christensen brothers gave me a scholarship to the school and a place in their ballet company. At last I began to acquire a passable technique to go along with a natural ability to cover space and jump. It was a wonderful time of friendships, hard work, and a good feeling of accomplishment.

At the end of three years I decided to try my luck in New York again. My heart was set on dancing with the New York City Ballet. Upon my arrival I requested an audition with Mr. Balanchine. He came to watch me take a pointe class. Later, Lincoln Kirstein told me that they would like to have me join the company, but that there wouldn't be an opening until their return from a six-month tour. I was thrilled about the future, but I had to get a job to tide me over financially and to feed my love of performing. So I danced in *Call Me Madam*, starring Ethel Merman. I was just assimilated into the show when a call came from the New York City Ballet saying that one of their dancers had had an appendectomy, and would I like to join the company for the grand tour. Would I! The following Sunday, my day off from *Call Me Madam*, I rushed to the City Center theatre to watch a performance of the ballet company, my future home. I arrived backstage fifteen minutes before curtain time to find an emergency rehearsal in progress for the first ballet, *Swan Lake*. Several of the corps members were out sick. The ballet mistress, Vida Brown, took one look at me in my healthy condition and said, 'We need you in this ballet company today!' I was still trying to comprehend what she meant as I was being whisked upstairs to the dressing room and pulled into pink tights. Someone pulled my hair back into a bun and stuck white feathers over my ears. Another dancer kept trying toe-shoes on my feet. It was decided that Tanaquil LeClercq's shoes were the best fit. By the time I reached the wings in full costume (but without makeup), the Prince and the Swan Queen were just finishing their first encounter on stage. Our music started and one of the swans said, 'Follow me.' I did. I was given instructions, what steps to dance and where to dance them, by the nearest swan. In what seemed like a few seconds, the Prince was kneeling in despair and the Swan Queen was exiting dramatically. Lots of hugs, smiles, and 'welcome to New York City Ballet' marked my most unusual entrance to the company. The following week I performed each night in *Madam*, trained my replacement for the show, found my birth certificate, got a passport, packed for the six-month tour, and flew off to Spain.

In the damp catacomb-like studio under the Liceo Theatre in Barcelona, I had my first class with Balanchine. It is etched in my mind forever. I was so astonished when he said I could raise my hip in arabesque and then, 'Don't try to get your heels down when you jump — just fly.' I knew I must be in heaven until he zeroed in on my feet and said, 'Turn out.' Once Mr. B. conjured up a vision of what you could be, he became a relentless taskmaster to that end. This was such a comforting environment in which to work; it kept at bay all doubts and questions of what to do and how to do it. I had complete faith in his vision and he was always there to tell you 'No not right, do again,' or 'Good dear, you see?'

The tour I joined in 1952 was fantastic. Europe was recovering from World War II. They had never seen the New York City Ballet. *Concerto Barocco, Symphony in C,* and *Serenade* were like a revelation to them, and we even shocked Paris dancing Jerome Robbins' *The Cage*. Seeing Europe was a dream come true, but it all had to be squeezed in between rehearsals. I had to learn the entire company repertoire as quickly as possible, and there were never enough dancers. Because I had gotten through my first performance of *Swan Lake* without a rehearsal, the ballet mistress decided I could follow my way through any ballet. I would find myself performing on the legendary Paris Opera stage with Igor Stravinsky conducting, or at the Royal Opera House at Covent Garden, with no clue in my head as to what the next dance step might be. Exciting times!

When we returned to the U.S., Mr. B. began using me in his new ballets. Going through the creative process of a new ballet with him was a unique experience. He knew what he wanted to say about the music and he knew every nuance of his dancers. This eliminated so much trial and error time. Some ballets he would choreograph as fast as we could learn the steps and the music. He was rarely demanding as to how you used your head or arms. He left breathing space in his choreography for the dancers to show their individuality. His ballets were never chiseled in stone and he was willing to change a variation to fit a newcomer. Mr. B. was always a gentleman, with those wonderful Old World manners. I always thought of him as a caring, nurturing, dictating father. I feel so fortunate to have been a part of that astonishing creative period of Balanchine's great genius.

The first role Mr. B. gave me was in the pas de trois in *Swan Lake*. In following years, he, Jerry Robbins, and guest choreographers gave me leading roles. I became an official soloist in 1954. Around the same time I began dating Jacques d'Amboise. On New Year's Day 1956 (the date chosen by Mr. B.), Jacques and I were married between matinee and evening performances of *The Nutcracker*. Our son George was born in November of the same year. It was not until 1958 that I rejoined the company during its four-month tour of Australia. On our return to America, our son had a life-threatening bout with cancer. George's illness made the decision to give up dancing for me. The suddenness of his illness, and the devastating prognosis, put the loss of my career into a different perspective. Compared to the loss of my son, the career was not worth a second thought. Without his illness, I'm sure I would have performed for many more years, as Mr. B. was quite determined to have me and I truly loved to dance. A year later our second son, Christopher, was born. George's cancer recurred, but after a second operation and X-ray treatment there was at last hope for him. The happy outcome is that he is now well and a wonderful thirty years old.

I think in most cases the transition from performer to mother is difficult. In the ballet world your responsibility is to yourself, and all your energies and concerns are self-directed. From my cloistered world of ballet I suddenly became responsible for a husband, four children (our twin daughters Charlotte and Kate were born in 1964), a house, finances, etc. I, as an individual, got lost in the shuffle. Today, miraculously, my children have all grown up. They are all wonderful people, busily working, happy, and my best friends. Now I feel I can be me again.

I read an article in a magazine that asked you to list your goals in order of priority. What a shock it was to realize I had no personal goals at all! I hadn't had one since I was a member of the New York City Ballet almost eighteen years ago. My first step in a personal direction was to get my body back into shape. Keeping up with our busy family had kept me slim, but the muscle tone was gone. I started teaching a dance-exercise class for neighborhood ladies. It has been a thrill for me to share in the fun of movement and to watch their amazing progress, but the most wonderful outcome has been the close friendships that have developed between us.

The second step I took was to enroll in the New School of Social Research. I took a variety of history and literature courses. My favorite was Chinese history. (I was hoping the New York City Ballet would someday go to China and that I could tag along with Jacques.) One term I took a darkroom photography class, just as a course filler. The first time I made a print from one of my negatives I was hooked. Watching the picture slowly develop was like a miracle. To practice the technique of photography I went home to the New York City Ballet. I made fast progress because I already had an understanding of the backstage workings and a knowledge of much of the choreography. Virginia Donaldson, head of the ballet's press department, used my better pictures for press releases and brochures. In 1981 there was an exhibition of my photographs at the Lincoln Center Gallery. I began getting jobs outside the ballet, photographing karate classes, off-Broadway theatre, or assignments from magazines, and pictures of my husband were always on demand. Simon and Schuster used seventy or eighty photographs for my husband's book *Teaching the Magic of Dance.* I also took photographs for my son Christopher's book, *Leap Year,* which told about his plunge into the world of the New York City Ballet from his days at Collegiate School. The School of American Ballet asked me to do a booklet for them. The school holds a special place in my heart, as Jacques and I and our four children all passed through the classes of those wonderfully dedicated teachers. Doing those photographs was a real labor of love.

My dream of going to China came true in 1984, when I toured for four weeks with a prominent writer, Barbara Goldsmith, taking photographs as she wrote her articles. They appeared in the *New York Times* and in *Parade* magazine. Then in 1985, I returned to China for a two-and-a-half-month stay. One of my assignments was to take photographs and to write an article on the Central Ballet of China for *Ballet News* publication. My early interest in China, years with the Ballet, and my career in photography all came together in this single project. I really felt I was the right person at the right time and place. My goal now is to get a book contract or a grant to return to China to photograph the old villages along the Three Gorge area of the Yangtse river, before they are submerged forever by a newly-planned dam.

One of the reasons I have been able to accomplish as much as I have in my second career of photography is that Jacques and my children have been completely supportive and excited about my photographs. Sometimes I think Jacques is a bit too prejudiced in my favor — but that's what makes him a great husband. In the early years there were a few complaints from my children ('Get out of the darkroom, Mom!'), but now they are very proud of my work. Our son George, after a four-year stint in the air force, is entering graduate school. Christopher is performing with the New York City Ballet and moonlighting in the Broadway musical *Song and Dance*, where he co-stars with Bernadette Peters. Charlotte left her first Broadway job in *Cats* to dance with her brother in *Song and Dance*. And Kate will be a senior at Denison University and spend summers working at a camp for children with learning disabilities.

I have had such a fortunate and wonderful life, and I owe much of it to my training as a dancer. Dancers have discipline and energy. Those two ingredients translate into success in any career. Add to that Mr. Balanchine's often-heard demand, 'Do it today like you are going to die tomorrow,' and you have an unbeatable combination."

# CHRISTOPHER DARLING

*"I think if you are searching for a new way of expression, or a new job, it is important to look within yourself, to look for the gift that you have been given and then try to express that gift with your highest ability."*

Photograph by Ken Bell

*Photograph by Marilyn Westlake*

*Christopher began his dance training in Phoenix while attending Arizona State University. His first performing experience was with the Arizona State modern dance group and the Phoenix Musical Theater. A year of intensive ballet training followed, during which time he met another dance student, Rebecca Bryan. They both moved to Toronto when offered scholarships at the National Ballet School. Rebecca soon became a member of the National Ballet of Canada, and after one year, Christopher joined the company.*

*While in Canada, Christopher and Rebecca were married and Christopher was drafted into the U.S. Army Infantry. Returning to the U.S. in 1969, he resumed his dancing with the Houston Ballet, and after six months joined the Royal Swedish Ballet, dancing with them for three years. While with that company, he mounted an exhibition of photography for the Swedish Government and decided to return to the U.S. to further his photographic work.*

*Christopher and Rebecca now live in Toronto and have three children. Christopher has worked as a freelance photographer for the National Ballet of Canada, the Canadian Broadcasting Corporation, the Hudson's Bay Company, and* The Globe and Mail. *He has produced a photographic book,* Kain and Augustyn, *published by Macmillan of Canada. For nearly five years, he worked as Director of Photography for Bata Limited, a large, multi-national shoe manufacturer. He recently resigned and plans to devote more time to his own creative projects in the future.*

"I was rather old by conventional standards when I became interested in ballet. I knew nothing about it until I was in my first year in political science at Arizona State University, where I began studying both modern dance and ballet. I had always been active in athletics, so the feeling of movement appealed to me. My first stage appearance was with the Arizona State modern dance group in a production of *Medea* when I was nineteen. I was the male lead surrounded by a bunch of diaphanous young creatures, and that whole thing kind of appealed to me. At the time I was told that I had a lot of talent and that I should continue. I took ballet classes in Phoenix and soon found myself dancing in a local production of *Oklahoma!*

The more I studied political science the less interested I became in pursuing it as a career, and dance became almost like an escape. My reason for choosing political science as a major was that I had traveled a lot in my life and the idea of being involved in international relations appealed to me. Of course the other reality was that I'd been going to school for fifteen years and was becoming rather bored with it. Some books that I ran across in the library about the old Diaghilev dancers, Nijinsky in particular, really fascinated me. I remember doing a term paper on him and even writing some poetry relating to ballet. I didn't know what I was getting into at that point, but I knew that I would need more training before I could consider becoming a professional. I was encouraged by my teachers, Bobby Lindgren and Sonja Tyven, and by some of my fellow dancers. In any event, I was really losing interest in my other studies by this time, and I went to New York to study ballet for a year. During the day I worked as a mail clerk in a newspaper office to pay for my studies. Then I met Rebecca Bryan, who later became my wife. She was also a ballet student, and shortly after I met her she was able to find a job with a small touring ballet company. During one of her tours she visited Toronto and made contact with the National Ballet School. We made arrangements to go up together to audition. Rebecca was accepted into the National Ballet company, and I became a scholarship student at the National Ballet School.

I remained there another year before joining the company. Because I had compressed what takes most people nine years to learn into such a short period of time, I don't think my dancing ever really became instinctive. I always had to concentrate very hard on what I was doing. That may have been my own ineptitude, or that I didn't have enough basic training. However, the feeling of moving through space with the music and having your body do all sorts of things that normal people couldn't do was exciting, and the lifestyle also seemed a bit glamorous. It was very hard work, but I loved the traveling. Seeing big cities and being on stage in front of an audience held a certain attraction for me. I think the opportunity to express something that people could appreciate and enjoy seeing was appealing. Even though I was in the corps de ballet during most of my career, it was a very nice experience to be working with other people, creating something that the audience could enjoy. I could, however, see the handwriting on the wall, and eventually decided that I wanted to get out while I could still adapt to a change of career.

Another problem was that this was during the Viet Nam war and, being a U.S. citizen, I was subject to the draft. I first received my draft notice when I was about twenty-three, and was able to obtain a deferment for a year. But finally I decided to enlist. During basic training I had an opportunity to apply to Officer Candidate School. I was accepted and completed the six-month course, became an infantry officer, and was then transferred to the Adjutant General's Corps, which is the administrative branch of the army. I turned in my M16 for a pen, and it seemed a lot nicer way to spend the next two years. The first year, I was in Montgomery, Alabama, at Maxwell Air Force Base in charge of Special Services for the army troops that were stationed there. Then for my last year, I was in Cam Rahn Bay, South Viet Nam, in a supply depot, again with Special Services. I had a pretty good assignment when you consider what I could have been doing at that point.

In 1969, I returned to the United States, was discharged, and tried to pick up the threads of my career. Rebecca had taken advantage of the interruption to have two of our children, so both of us had had three years off from ballet. We moved to Houston, Texas, and tried to pick up where we left off. Houston had a small ballet company, the Houston Ballet, which has now grown into quite a nice regional company. At that time, they were desperately in need of male dancers and I had not done a barre in three years. So, two weeks after moving to Houston I was learning some of the repertoire and within about a month I was on stage again.

I had been very active in the military and was always in very good shape. We had had quite a strenuous physical training program and, in fact, during basic training at Fort Dix, New Jersey, I became the first person in my unit to ever get a perfect score on the Physical Combat Proficiency Test. We stayed with the Houston Ballet about six months and, while we were there, decided to try to join an opera-ballet company in Europe. The companies in Europe tend to be more family-oriented and they don't tour quite as much. We went to New York and auditioned for the Royal Swedish Ballet. They had an opening for male dancers only, and I was one of the dancers they selected. We decided to go and in the second year Rebecca was asked to join the company. For the next two years we both danced together with the Royal Swedish Ballet under Erik Bruhn's direction. This was one of the greatest periods of growth in my career as a dancer. I had opportunities to work with some very exciting choreographers and to dance in many full-length productions.

I had majored in photography as part of an art course in high school, and, while I took pictures of dancers quite early in my dance career, I didn't have anything published until I moved to Sweden, where my interest in photography began to revive. I was doing quite a bit of photography for the company and was asked to do an exhibition for the Swedish government. When I began making money at photography, I began to see that perhaps there was another way to go. I was getting a lot of recognition in my work as a photographer, which eased the transition from dance to photography.

Many of the principles that are used in ballet are also applicable to photography. You're dealing with movement, rhythm, composition and grace, and many other elements. What distinguishes one dancer from another? There's a certain intangible quality, a certain excitement, in seeing a great dancer do even a simple step. I think you can see that same quality in a great photograph. Sometimes it's very hard to say exactly what it is; it's a certain element that strikes your fancy. To borrow an idea from a famous photographer, Henri Cartier-Bresson, the important thing is to capture the decisive moment. Certainly in dance photography, timing is everything; to be able to capture the peak of the movement requires a sensitivity and an awareness of the movement itself, and some training in the art form.

Ultimately, we decided as a family that we didn't want to remain in Sweden for the rest of our lives. We'd had an opportunity to really enjoy living and working there, but it was time to go home. I wanted to pursue my career as a photographer and Rebecca wanted to devote more of her time to raising the children. I applied for an opening in a very good school of photography in Santa Barbara, California, called the Brooks Institute. I was accepted and we moved to Santa Barbara with the intention of my becoming a student there. That didn't work out because we simply didn't have the funds to send me through three years of school. There was no way we could survive, so I ended up going to Santa Barbara City College for six months. Then, an opportunity to work with the United States International University in San Diego presented itself and we moved to San Diego. I enrolled in Grossmont Junior College as a communications major and took courses related to photography, audio-visual production and graphic arts.

At that time I really became involved professionally and started doing freelance assignments for the Old Globe Theatre in San Diego — an audio-visual production, a lot of portraitures and portfolios for up-and-coming actors and dancers. There really wasn't a very big market in San Diego for theatrical photography, but I did the best I could and we got by. At this point we thought that maybe Toronto had something to offer us and during the summer of 1972 we came back to Canada. Although we'd been gone for seven years, we found that we still had a lot of contacts in Toronto. I was offered a job at a photographic studio. Later, my wife was offered a position on the staff of the National Ballet School. Eventually I started freelancing. I got my own studio and began to acquire my own clients, mainly from the contacts that I'd previously made as a dancer.

I had photographed Karen Kain and Frank Augustyn quite a bit and realized that I had hundreds of photographs of them. I contacted a publisher who expressed interest in doing a book, and it happened very, very quickly. The timing was perfect. I had the goods and they thought it was marketable. It was called, *Kain and Augustyn* and it sold well over 15,000 copies in Canada and the United States. It was also published and sold in the United Kingdom and I made quite a bit of money from it, enough to feel that I had achieved a certain amount of success. It gave me a lot more confidence and opened a few doors, so that my business began to grow.

I'd been involved in a few different areas of photography, and I realized pretty early in my career as a theatrical photographer that it was not very remunerative. The book was certainly a financial success and I hope somewhat of an artistic success, but when the money from the royalties stops, you still have to live. Also, most of the performers who were using my services couldn't afford to pay a lot of money for the work I was doing. I began to get involved in other areas of photography and I worked regularly for such clients as the Canadian Broadcasting Corporation, the National Ballet, the Hudson's Bay Company and *The Globe and Mail*. I began developing many commercial accounts, doing anything from publicity and fashion to magazine, book, and album covers, as well as advertising and catalogue photography, and won art directors awards for some of my work. Eventually I became Director of Photography for Bata Limited, a multi-national corporation where I remained for nearly five years before returning to freelance photography. I would like to be able to continue with photography, but to devote more time to my own creative projects such as photographic books.

I think we all have something that is unique about us. I've been trying for many years to discover what it is in me that I have to give. I guess you could say I'm ambitious. I've always been very responsive to my environment, and I've soaked up everything around me wherever I've been. I enjoy people, and I hope that I can share a unique vision of life through my photographic projects in future years.

In life we start out with a dream or a goal, and little by little things happen to us, circumstances affect us, so that we're often not able to express what we really want to express. We have to live. We get married, have children and financial responsibilities. These weigh heavily on the creative person, and it is important not to lose the ability to dream.

I think if you are searching for a new way of expression or a new job, it is important to look within yourself, to look for the gift that you have been given and then try to express that gift with your highest ability. This can be a very difficult process and sometimes you may have to go through quite a long transitional period to discover your true gift. I think the idea of having a gift is something very profound. Life is in reality a gift from God. A lot of us are guilty of just accepting circumstances and not pursuing the dream that we once had. Every change must be progressive to be right. What I would say to anyone going through this transitional period is to recognize that the present is all that really exists. Look back, not to look at what's been done, but to try to recapture the reality — the dream that was once there."

# MARIAN HOROSKO

*"If you do decide to stop dancing, don't mourn the loss of your dance   career because it isn't lost. It is still within you, and the qualities   that were developed and the talents you had for that career are still  there. They're just going to blossom in another way."*

*Photograph by Maurice Seymour*

Photograph by Kenn Duncan

## EXCHANGES: LIFE AFTER DANCE

*Marian began her ballet studies in Cleveland, Ohio. As a student, she gave her first performance with the Ballet Russe de Monte Carlo, before going to New York City. She immediately found a job at Radio City Music Hall while continuing with her dance and piano studies. Marian performed on Broadway in several musicals including* Oklahoma!, *and in films such as* Royal Wedding, An American in Paris, *and* The Prince Who Was a Thief. *She danced with the Metropolitan Opera Ballet from 1950 to 1954, becoming a soloist before joining the New York City Ballet in 1954 and dancing with them until 1961.*

*Since leaving that company, Marian has worked extensively in both radio and television programming. More than 350 tapes of her weekly radio interview show have since been acquired by the Dance Collection of the New York Public Library at Lincoln Center. Since 1959, she has been a contributing editor and is now associate editor of* Dance Magazine, *and has written two books on Soviet ballet technique* (Pas de Deux, *based upon Serrebrenikov, and* Ballet Technique for the Male Dancer, *based upon pedagogue Nikolai Tarasov). She is currently working on a book for Harper and Row with Judith Kupersmith, M.D., on the psychological problems of performing. She has also taught at the High School for the Performing Arts and at Fordham University and became the first film archivist for the Dance Collection at Lincoln Center. With Kupersmith, she is one of the founders of the Performing Arts Center for Health in New York City.*

"I was encouraged to appreciate all the arts right from the beginning. I studied dance in Cleveland, Ohio, with Serge Nadejdin, who had danced with the Pavlova Company and had studied in St. Petersburg (Leningrad). In our school we had the opportunity to watch every visiting company rehearse, so we saw nothing but good dancing. We had no other influences whatsoever. Nadejdin was a fine pianist, a graduate of the Maryinsky school in dance and music. He gave us not super-technical training, but a great love for dance and everything related to the arts. We went to the symphony and the museum, and had an exceptional education for the Midwest in the thirties when nobody else in that area of the country was getting that kind of education.

I think the big difference in the training now is that today's dancers are trained to have a career. We were trained to have a profession and a profession is a way of life. It has no hours and no limits on its interest, and it puts no limits upon you and what you are called upon to do. A career has what they call upward mobility, goals, income requirements, and it's a job. It involves competitiveness and all the social standards of its time. I don't know what that means. Dance has not left me and I have not left dance. It's still part of my background. It's part of what I see and hear, the way I look at things, the way I move. It's the way I dress. It hasn't gone out of my life. It's just found another place to go.

When I was sixteen, I danced with Pittsburgh Civic Light Opera. It was fun. After that I went to New York and began my life in professional dance. When my mother brought me to New York, she said, 'We have six months, and if you don't get a job by then you can't go on the stage.' In two weeks I was in Radio City Music Hall. I didn't want to waste any time! I took the opportunity to study with many individual teachers. When I went to class, I used to stand at the barre with tears in my eyes because I couldn't believe that all these extraordinary people were standing next to me. And the music was so wonderful. That's another thing that is often missing now. The musician's contribution to a class should be a collaboration, not just an accompaniment.

Class was exciting and exhausting, and there was no such thing as two classes. You could hardly get through one! It gave you musicianship, versatility, quickness of mind, and a huge range of possibilities. We all went to Mme. Anderson. She was strict, rigid, and technically correct, and was extremely demanding about a critical classical style. We used to find different teachers for different things because we didn't have it all in one school.

I stayed at Radio City and, at the same time, went to Juilliard during the day to study piano. I didn't like Juilliard because they put me in what I called 'baby classes,' and didn't recognize credits I already had. So I decided to go to Columbia University and continue my piano studies there. Then I heard that there was an opening in *Oklahoma!* I auditioned to replace Diana Adams and got the job. I remember Agnes DeMille once saying to me that I was the antithesis of what she wanted as a dancer in the company. When I met her recently, I reminded her of that remark and told her that I had tried to live up to that for the rest of my life!

Eventually, I went to Hollywood at the invitation of Nick Castle. I did the ending of a film called *Royal Wedding* with Fred Astaire and Jane Powell, and then somebody on that set saw me and asked me to do *An American in Paris*. I made three more movies in that year, but what I wanted was to try to get into the Metropolitan Opera Ballet in New York or stop dancing entirely, because the whole commercial world was not what I wanted.

I came back to New York, got into the Met, and became a soloist there for three years. It was the happiest job I ever had. I was married at the time to pianist Jacob Lateiner. Jacob was an enormous talent. The problem was that we were both too successful, and I think we were too successful at a time when neither of us knew how to handle it. Success is much headier than failure and we had no one to guide us. We didn't know how to spend or use money and we didn't know how to budget. We were extravagant and ridiculous, but I adored him. Everything he said was all right with me and he didn't know how to handle this kind of headiness either. It was a question of success coming too fast. Practicing became difficult for him, and then Jacob stopped practicing and playing altogether and went to see a psychiatrist. Eventually we separated. I had always hoped to get back together. I went to a psychiatrist for a while, too, and got back some of my self-esteem, individuality, and independence. We never did get together again, which is unfortunate because I think we had the makings of a very good relationship.

At the Met, my partner was Roland Vazquez and we had decided that we should try to get into the New York City Ballet. One day between La Traviata and the next opera, Roland and I went over to the New York City Ballet and danced for Mr. Balanchine. We did the only thing we knew, which was the second act of La Traviata, and we both got in!

The New York City Ballet was a revelation. Balanchine's intellectual capacity, his versatility, his musicianship, the excitement of every day, the challenges, the company as a family, and the traveling were very different from my previous experiences. People were more varied and versatile and the atmosphere was totally different. In the New York City Ballet there was a lot more co-operation. Relationships with each other were more supportive and at the same time it was much more challenging.

Eventually I left the company because I had an injury, and I had to do something immediately because I had no way to live. I had written some articles for Dance Magazine while still in the company and so I had some previous writing experience. It didn't make the transition any easier, however. I think loss of career is similar to loss of a loved one. It is a death. The first thing that happens is anger. Why me? The next thing is depression and then acceptance. When you get to the acceptance stage, it doesn't mean you are not depressed or angry at various times in your life; it means that you have come to terms with it, and you realize that what you got in dance as a professional will stand by you in many other situations. People see that you have qualitites that they want: contacts, self-reliance, independence, creativity, and so on.

I used to have two or three jobs at the same time. That's the way I like to live. I wrote press releases, articles for *Dance Magazine* and, after a while, I worked for WNET, the public television station, eventually becoming an Assistant Producer. I also started a radio show because there was a strike on at the *New York Times* and there were no reviews being published. At one point I walked into the radio station WNCN and I said, 'Listen, there's nobody to cover these performances.' Nobody was doing reviews. And that's how my radio interview show started. I did it for seventeen years. I interviewed everybody in the music and dance world. Those interviews were like overheard conversations in the Russian Tearoom, and seventeen years later they found their way into the dance archives of the New York Public Library at Lincoln Center.

To make a living, I was working at WNET and at the Lena Robbins Film Archives of the Dance Collection at the New York Public Library. Later, I became Head of Film Archives for the library. I was still working for *Dance Magazine* as a contributing editor. I also wrote a book on Soviet ballet technique. That started at *Dance Magazine* as a series on all the Russians who came to America about the same time as Mr. Balanchine did. They came to America and had to teach but didn't know how. They were still performers. It was a tragedy because they had nowhere to perform. They were first-rate dancers and there was nothing for them to do but just stop.

I also did some teaching at the High School of Performing Arts and at Fordham University, but I didn't enjoy it. At Fordham, absenteeism was high and it was too late to teach them anything. And at P.A., the students were more interested in the dance schools they attended after P.A.

Then I had an experience which completely changed my life. I was in Buffalo staging *Coppelia*. I was walking along the New York Thruway in eight degrees below zero weather with the actor who played Dr. Coppelius. We were walking on the wrong side of the Thruway because we were afraid the cars were going to come out too fast from an entrance ramp. It was very cold and windy and he was in front of me. As we were walking I said to him, 'Let's change places because I know the way.' We had just changed places and I was walking in front. I turned around to say something and he was gone. I thought he was kidding. There were some oil drums along the side of the road and I thought he was hiding. After a few minutes I got a little angry because I couldn't find him anywhere and I said, 'Okay, I'm leaving. I'm freezing cold. I'll see you at the motel.' As I started to walk away a car came along, and as the headlights hit the center of the road I saw his body. He had been hit just as we were changing places.

He lived, but it was touch and go. I had three days without sleep or food. I couldn't close my eyes without seeing his body. It was my luck not to be the one hit. He was a great big guy and he survived, but if it had been me, that would have been it. The accident changed my life, and I decided that every day was going to be the day that I wanted it to be, and that's true to this day. I will dare anything, say anything, do anything — because life itself is more important than the career, the money, what you do, what anybody thinks, or what anybody says about you.

As a result, I didn't apply for a job that had money, and I didn't go for so-called career security. I started a cable show which failed, although it won a prize for one of the ten best cable shows of the year. I lost everything I had in the bank. The show was about cultural subjects and it was a little too soon for cable. I think the lesson to be learned here is that I got back into life with the same vitality I'd had in the ballet. Dance is real; it's thinking, feeling, and being conscious. I think now I'm back in the real world and that means that I'm willing to cope with anything that comes along.

My next job was with a magazine. It was a terrific job for a French fashion magazine, but no sooner did I get that job than the magazine went bankrupt. I was doing dance and health in a fashion and beauty magazine. So I said, 'Why not health and beauty in a dance magazine?' I spoke to the editor of *Dance Magazine*, and I started to do a regular column. I found I could help in tangible ways. For instance, we did a series of articles on drugs. As a result of these articles we contacted doctors who were sympathetic to dance. The atmosphere of suspicion between the medical profession and dance seemed to be breaking down. We decided to form an organization which would provide information for the prevention of injuries and offer pre-diagnostic services, including a referral service of doctors across the country who would not put you in psychological jeopardy by saying, 'Why don't you stop?' Also at that time, I met Judy Kupersmith, a former dancer with the New York City Ballet who is now a psychiatrist, and we started a series on emotional problems — things we wished we had known how to handle twenty years ago. The result was the establishment of the Performing Arts Center for Health. It was the right thing at the right time and the right place.

First we did a survey of two hundred and eighteen professional companies in the New York City area, from which we got a one hundred company response. We discovered that some of the problems experienced were in physical areas that we didn't know about: dental care, massage and physical therapy, gynecology, eye disorders, chiropractic and orthopedic services. We also found that the emotional needs of dancers are very strong. Dancers are becoming integrated into society, and they have to cope with the outside world as well as with their conditioning as performers. One has to differentiate between the conditioning one gets at home, in society, and in the media, and the conditioning one gets in the career.

Some of the problems can be solved within the career. For instance, the loneliness problem does not have to exist if there is no fear of intimate relationships which can teach about feelings. The problem of depression perhaps need not exist if it isn't analyzed as depression. It may simply be a need for rest. The stress of traveling doesn't have to be stress, although the pace is faster now and it's a little harder on the body. There are more opportunities to meet people now. A dancer can enlarge and expand his or her willingness to relate. Competition is a bigger problem in dance companies now. Dancers are perceiving their careers as seven years long, and this is ridiculous for the amount of training and effort involved. Competition really only exists within oneself.

I would say to dancers, if you do decide to stop dancing, don't mourn the loss of your dance career because it isn't lost. It is still within you, and the qualities that were developed and the talents you had for that career are still there. They're just going to blossom in another way. There is not one person in this world with only one talent, and it is only our negative thoughts and fears that keep us from blossoming in other areas. What dancers have to discover is what their other talents are.

I think the big problem in transition is to realize that there is a lot of mediocrity out there, and there are a lot of people who are not qualified to do what they are doing. You have been trained to be good at every performance. There is no tomorrow and no yesterday.

There's only today, and what you do every single time you are out there has to be in full consciousness and your best work, or else you don't have a job the next time. This is not always true in other things.

I think what has happened in the dance world since I was dancing is that there has been a greater concentration and focus on getting to a career, on advancing and getting all your technique at one time. This has not allowed the dancer to grow psychologically and emotionally. This is where one has to catch up. If dancers will just continue that openness and willingness to learn and grow, I think they can make a wonderful contribution. They don't have to be afraid that they haven't got that degree, diploma, or other training. They have the equal of that, and I think they have to trust and go along with the job or the challenge being offered. The problem is feeling that one is no longer unique because something has been lost. That is the big problem, and that's a spiritual and emotional matter. It really has nothing to do with career. It's recreating your inner life by shoring up your problems and your strengths.

For us dancing was a way of life. If it's only a career, then you haven't gained as much joy from it as you could have and you haven't enriched yourself. I think the worst thing in life is not to take the risks, and not to accept the challenges, and not to make that total commitment. Total involvement is a contribution. When your commitment is not total, it's riding along on the efforts of other people, on the gifts of other people, on the involvement of other people. It's very much on the surface. The growth of dance has been made possible by people who were willing to risk and go all the way whatever the cost.

The times have done one thing for us: they have made dance accessible to everyone, which is good. The things that Mr. Balanchine taught us: structure, reaching a high point, commitment, concentration, being present, being aware — all those things are there to be used and applied to the next thing you do. It's all a performance and all life is a risk."

# CHARLES KIRBY

*"At some point, I realized I was getting older! Sometimes a dancer has to shake himself and say, 'There is a tomorrow,' and do something about it!"*

*Photograph by Andrew Oxenham*

Photograph by David Street

Charles was born in Little Rock, Arkansas, and was involved in drama and musical productions throughout school and college there. In 1945 he won his college choreographic competition and set and theatre model design awards. After graduating with an Associate of Arts degree from Little Rock Junior College, he went to New York and studied ballet with Vera Nemtchinova and Aubrey Hitchins. In 1946 he went to Los Angeles to study with Bronislava Nijinska, before returning to Little Rock to assist in forming and directing a concert dance group, the Ballet Society of Arkansas. He taught, choreographed, and performed extensively in Arkansas and later in Memphis, co-directing the Memphis Civic Ballet and opening schools in both Little Rock and Memphis. Charles joined the National Ballet of Canada in 1965, becoming a soloist in 1972 and a principal dancer in 1976. He has also taught company classes at the National Ballet and was the director of their Prologue to the Performing Arts program.

He has choreographed for CBC television, the Canadian Opera Company, and the National Arts Centre in Ottawa, and has been Ballet Master for a National Ballet concert group. He has served on the advisory board of George Brown College in Toronto and on the executive board of the Canadian Actors' Equity Association. He is also co-owner of a Toronto restaurant, Abundance, which opened in January of 1980. Charles continues to perform principal character roles for the National Ballet of Canada.

"If I was interested in movement, it had to be because I thought Fred Astaire and Ginger Rogers were the greatest things since cream cheese! I saw all their movies as a child in Little Rock, Arkansas. By my teens, I knew I wanted to do something in the theatre, but my family worried about my happiness and my security. I didn't even start studying dance until my last year in high school.

I studied with a local teacher, Mildred Reamey, and accompanied some classes for her as I could play the piano. After high school, I entered college as a pre-med student to satisfy my parents, but I attended for only two years. Then I said, 'Okay, now it's my turn.' I was still thinking of a theatrical career, but I hadn't decided if I was going to sing, dance, or be an actor. I did know, however, that I would be one of the three.

I went to New York where I studied with Vera Nemtchinova and Aubrey Hitchins. After a few months of study I developed pneumonia and had to go home. When I regained my health, I went to California and studied with Mme. Nijinska. Her classes were full of energy and vigor, but probably still in the back of my mind I had the thought,

'Well, if a movie job comes along, I'll take it.'

While I was in California, I received a call from Joy Shoemaker, a girl with whom I'd done some ballroom dancing in Little Rock. She had been studying in New York all this time, and she said, 'I've met a ballet master/choreographer, Manolo Agullo, and we've decided to put together a concert dance group. Can you come and do it with us?' I had a job in California working in public relations for Mutual Broadcasting, but when Joy called the idea seemed interesting. So I went back to Little Rock and tried to form a concert dance company. What an idealist!

In fact, putting that group together was just miserable, miserable work. It was like beating your head against a stone wall. We discovered that we couldn't make a living because we couldn't get enough shows, and if you couldn't get the shows you couldn't pay the bills. Our families were supporting us but the difficulty with that was that we felt tied to them; you're back home and you feel worthless because you can't do it on your own. We finally realized that we had to do something to declare our independence. What we did was to open a school in competition with Mildred Reamey. It was a tiny school and it didn't work out well. I was also performing in musicals and our dance group still gave concerts. Around this time, we were offered a school in Memphis, Tennessee. We took over that school and we started another concert group. Then we started a regional group, the Memphis Civic Ballet, which became part of the Southeastern Regional Ballet Festival Association.

At that time, I was the right age to do it. The work load was enormous, but when you're young you have health. You think you can afford to give it away and you do. You will work eighteen-hour days as a director of a regional company. No one helps you. If you want to put on a show, you have to realize that you're going to do it yourself. Of course, Manolo and myself were joint directors, so I wasn't completely alone, and Joy continued to teach at the school for two years. We did everything for this company. I choreographed eighteen original ballets, designed and made costumes, constructed scenery, and danced. We all made an enormous contribution.

Eventually, however, I had to get out. I had let myself become engulfed. I was trying to run this company as professionally as possible. We were doing ballets for the opera company and dances for the musical theatre, and I was trying to teach students from age six up. I was teaching everybody, giving to everybody. I suddenly said, 'It's my turn now.' That's why I came to Canada. A job happened to be available at the National Ballet of Canada.

I was enormously impressed with Celia Franca. I didn't have to make decisions anymore. I had to do it her way, which was exactly what I wanted at the time. This woman was a dynamo and I deeply respected her. Soon, however, the situation changed. Celia asked me to take on the Prologue to the Performing Arts program, an introduction to the performing arts presented in Ontario schools, which had started out as an idea developed by a group of volunteers who supported the symphony, opera, ballet, and theatre. This group had decided that the time had come in Toronto to expose younger children to these forms in order to further develop audiences. The first thing they did was put together a group of attractions that they were then able to offer to school boards. The school boards within the city then bought these shows and could choose any combination of them they wished. I was asked to choreograph and be Ballet Master for this group. I did have fun with that because it allowed me to use my creativity without the stress I'd experienced in Memphis. We participated in Prologue for five or six years, and then our regular performing schedule became too heavy and we couldn't accept further engagements.

During this time, my career was also evolving from corps de ballet dancer to my present position of principal character artist. My body has been good to me. There are not many people who joined a ballet company at age thirty-nine as a corps de ballet dancer. I'm not unusual; what has happened to me is unusual. I've noticed there are similarities of nature among character artists. To begin with, we are all at home with the grand gesture. It's very natural for us. It comes out of our bodies easily. As people, we are open, warm conversationalists, and yet retiring and private. In other words, we seem to have a certain insecurity, but we're not afraid on stage. We're not afraid of looking ugly and we're not afraid of looking handsome. I think that's how you have to be for character work.

At some point, I realized I was getting older! Sometimes a dancer has to shake himself and say, 'There is a tomorrow,' and do something about it! A small incident proved to be a turning point for me. I was at a party and, needless to say, there was food and drink. A group of us proceeded to discuss how poor the food preparation was. One particular person in this group and I began to joke about hamburgers. We'd rather have had a hamburger than this fancy stuff that had been

90

prepared. This person, Jacques Wensvoort, became my partner. We discovered that we had great similarities in taste. He is an excellent cook, and I'm told I'm a good cook. I have always enjoyed giving dinner parties. I take pride in presenting an elaborate table for twelve, serving three wines and all that business. I mean, that's fun!

I realized that if I was going to do anything towards my future, I needed to make a commitment somewhere and this looked like a good opportunity. I knew the ability of the person who would become my partner. I knew what we were about and I trusted our taste. I also knew that by going into the restaurant business I could rely on the people who had come to see me perform, the people from the opera company where I choreographed, and on those from television and so forth, to be my patrons. I felt that perhaps I had a built-in patronage because I was a 'personality' in the theatre. Even so, it took a lot to get a restaurant opened: negotiating with banks, business men, supply companies, setting up credit references, all of that.

Abundance, our restaurant, opened on January 18, 1980, and was very successful until April 6, 1982. That morning, the place was destroyed by fire. The Fire Marshal's report indicated that it had been caused by old wiring in the building. Of course, at the time, the fire was devastating. We just watched all that work burn up. But we set to planning the new restaurant on the day of the fire and the new Abundance opened on April 25, 1983, just around the corner from the old location.

The concept of Abundance stayed the same. It's based on food that is wholesome, fresh, and freshly prepared. Even if it's dessert, it's made from scratch and it's made with good stuff. That's really what my partner and I want to do. We're both concerned with waste in the world and we're concerned about additives in food. We try to get the best. If you come to us and you want orange juice, it's freshly squeezed. It's not out of a can and it isn't frozen. I think we've been successful.

As for my performing career, when you've been in any career as long as I have, you might realize it's going to be difficult to walk away from it — to not put on those shoes one more time. I have a few close friends in the company, and I imagine I would still see them occasionally if I stopped performing, but I don't know — it's hard to say. Another consideration, of course, is the performing itself. I think that's one of the things I would miss the most. After all, it's why you're there in the first place. You can't just suddenly close yourself up! With the restaurant, however, I'm still in front of the public. I think it's important to look at yourself and try to find out what you think you do well, and if it's something you enjoy, the road will be easier. In my case, it was all very natural in the way that it happened and I think that, knowing me, I might have taken a different highway to the same place. Dancers have intelligence and ability — they just need a direction."

# JUDITH KUPERSMITH

*"There is life after dance! If we want young dancers to mature and become healthy adults, they have to think about such things. If such thinking is discouraged by people around them, there's no reason for them to face it. If it is encouraged and given a more positive profile, it can only be of benefit to the individual."*

*Photograph by Martha Swope*

*Photographer Unknown*

*Judy began ballet and piano studies in New York. Her first dance classes were with Dorothy Bird and subsequently at the School of American Ballet. She graduated from High School in 1957 and entered Hunter College. After only one month of college, she was invited to be an apprentice with the New York City Ballet. In February 1958, Judy was accepted into the company just prior to their six-month tour of Japan, Australia, and Manila. She danced with them for five years, and during that time also performed as piano soloist in Balanchine's* Liebeslieder Walzer.

*After leaving the company in 1962, Judy re-entered Hunter College, graduating in 1964. She was then accepted into New York Medical College and graduated with an M.D. in 1969. She completed her internship in pediatrics at the Metropolitan Hospital and Medical Center, New York, before deciding to specialize in psychiatry. In 1973 she completed a three-year residency in psychiatry at Boston City Hospital. Judy has been Assistant Attending Psychiatrist at New York University Medical Center since 1973, Assistant Clinical Professor of Psychiatry at New York University School of Medicine since 1978, and, also since 1978, Assistant Attending Psychiatrist, Bellevue Hospital. There she helped to establish the Performing Arts Center for Health, serving the special health needs of performing artists. Judy is married to Dr. Joel Kupersmith, and, with him and their three children, Adam, David, and Rebecca, has recently moved to Louisville, Kentucky, where she will establish a Performing Arts Center for Health in the medical services department of the University of Louisville.*

"I loved to dance. I loved the feel of it and I looked forward to classes; this was what I wanted to do. Everything else came second, even the piano which was so important to me. I remember going to school wearing my leotard and tights underneath my other clothes. I couldn't wait until the bell rang and class was let out. Everybody else would get up slowly and walk out the door. I ran. I was running to ballet class. I liked the discipline and the work. I never got bored with a class even in those early years when classes were so repetitive. To me it was always a new, fresh, wonderful experience. It wasn't until later years, after other conflicts had started to move in, that I began looking at the clock, getting bored, wondering when it was going to be over. In the student days, that never happened because of this great love for dance.

I started ballet classes at the YMHA (Young Men's Hebrew Association) on 92nd Street with Dorothy Bird, who sent me to Doris Humphrey after a year. Doris Humphrey thought I would be very well suited to dance, but I didn't like her type of dance. Eventually, she referred me to the School of American Ballet. From the minute I walked into that school, I felt I had found a home. My teachers there left a great impression on me. The first one that comes to mind is Madame Tumkovsky. She was not my first teacher but she was the one who had the most effect on me, and I think the reason was her enthusiasm, concern, and commitment to the individual dancer. She had very strong feelings about talented dancers who worked hard. She was appreciative and rational, and I responded very well to that. I'm sure that's why I remember her so well, although there were many other teachers from whom I learned a great deal.

I was studying the piano at the same time. There was a lot of competition and conflict within myself. I couldn't decide which to do, whether to go with music or dance, and at that particular time I didn't want to give up either. I felt if I wasn't able to do the one I'd do the other. Occasionally there would be some conflict about it, but I always found time to practice the piano an hour and a half a day and to take my daily ballet class. I think they enhanced each other, but somewhere along the way I realized that there was more of a chance for me to be professional in dance rather than music. I really didn't feel I was good enough to become a concert pianist, although I did play some concerts.

In June of 1957 I graduated from high school. I worked very hard in my ballet classes over that summer with the hope of getting into the New York City Ballet, because that would have saved me from going to college. My parents were making it quite clear that if I didn't get into the company I'd have to go to college, and that was not something I wanted to do. September rolled around, I was not in the company, and so I enrolled in college, majoring in music. I went to classes for a month or so, and then I was invited to be an apprentice with the company for that Fall season. Of course I dropped my books with a great bang and happily took the apprenticeship. When that was finished, I was not invited to join the company right away. Once again, the next semester rolled around and my parents were on my back: 'You're not in the company, Judy. You've got to go to college.' So I enrolled again in January, but in February I got a phone call saying that the New York City Ballet was going on a six-month tour of Japan, Australia, and Manila and would I like to join? Once again, I dropped my books, got my passport, and left.

It was my first season as a member of the New York City Ballet. We were thousands of miles away in Japan, a land where I did not speak the language, and it was the first time I had been away from home. I had been thrown into the company on very short notice. Even the picture in the souvenir book had my face on somebody else's body because there wasn't enough time to make a whole new picture. And that's pretty much what I felt like when I arrived in Japan: I had a head, but the rest wasn't quite attached!

I have many memories of that first season in Japan. Although I thought of myself as a fast learner and thought I could quickly integrate and assimilate what was expected of me, it was a very stressful and chaotic time. The other aspect of that first season being so far away had to do with the personal side: making friends, establishing roommates, finding out what your roommates liked and didn't like, and all of this with the overtone that you had to perform every night. It was very traumatic and took a lot of growing up, and, within a very short period of time, I developed every possible neurosis and psychological problem that could be related to these stresses. The dedication and discipline of hard work seemed to ebb, and I felt very disturbed by this. I couldn't understand why I wasn't giving it my all. Basically, the stress was too great for me at that particular time.

As the months passed, there were periods when I felt very dedicated and I was able to work hard and to do my best. But those periods never lasted very long. I'm a very compulsive, hard-working person, and not to be like that was very disturbing. Yet I found it happening and I really didn't know how to deal with it.

One of my most memorable experiences was when Mr. Balanchine invited me to play one of the piano parts for *Liebeslieder Walzer*, while I was still a member of the company. It was a wonderful learning experience for me to participate in this type of professional performance. However, it didn't do anything for my feelings about myself as a dancer. Playing was a talent that I had, and I felt I could do both things kind of halfway. I still wasn't doing the dancing full out. There was something stopping me throughout all those years. I never fully understood it, and to this day there are times when I feel that I really did have the talent and that I really could have succeeded with dance, but my emotional conflicts were so great that there was no way I could have surmounted them.

The last season I was with the company, I was depressed and functioning poorly. Part of my personality at that time was very passive: 'Let's wait and see what happens (let's see how we can destroy

98

ourselves enough before somebody on the outside lets the axe come down)." I finally received a letter from Mr. Balanchine saying that although we like you very much and you're a nice person and a nice dancer, we can't continue with you the way things are right now, which I understood very well. I filed that letter away. It's always had a very special meaning for me. Later I realized that my dancing career had come to an end at that point and there was no way I could have resurrected it, but at the time, I felt very much a failure. Part of my personality was very obsessive, compulsive, and hard-working, so I went to school almost within a week of leaving the New York City Ballet. The next six months were probably the worst time of my life, even though I had the safety and security of going to school.

The transition from being in Balanchine's company to becoming a freshman in a city college was traumatic. I didn't want to see or talk to anybody. Finally, in a state of tremendous unhappiness, I asked my father if he knew the name of a psychiatrist that I could see. My father was an internist. He had always been very supportive of my dancing and my music, and I know he must have experienced a lot of disappointment when I gave them up. But he was supportive enough to recognize that there were other things that I could do, and if I needed help in the form of a psychiatrist or whatever, he would support me both emotionally and financially. It was then that I started therapy.

My father recommended a Freudian analyst. I had difficulties engaging in that kind of therapy and in feeling that I was getting anything out of it. I really just needed someone to talk to, someone who could be very direct and help me see the reality of my situation. When I became fully aware of the state I was in and realized how badly I had reacted to everything, it became very important for me to succeed in something, and with my father being a physician and my mother a teacher, there was a strong pull towards the academic life. Because of the encouragement of my father, the field of medicine became more and more attractive.

The whole undergraduate college experience lasted only two and a half years, and it really couldn't have taken more than six or eight months before I decided that I was going to become a doctor and that I wanted to be a psychiatrist. When I was accepted into medical school I burst into tears, and my family didn't understand. I felt that I wouldn't be able to do it. However, I persevered, did succeed, and I've had a very wonderful life ever since.

The discipline of dance taught me something invaluable. Once I got into medical school I was in a completely different environment. I found that I could sit for long periods of time and that I could concentrate. There was a dedication, a sense of purpose, a set of goals to be achieved, just as I had had with dancing.

I graduated from medical school in 1969 and did an internship for one year in pediatrics because, after having put four years into medical school, I had started to change my mind a little about psychiatry. I felt that pediatrics was a science and that I should stay in the scientific area — so I decided to try it. After a few months, I realized that my original plan was a lot better and I went back into psychiatry. In 1973 I completed my three-year residency period, so I've been a practicing psychiatrist now for thirteen years.

When I completed my residency, I believed that I was never going to go back to dancing again. I felt that there could be no connection between the two and that the dance world was a thing of the past. But then, as time went on, I began to see that I could utilize elements from the past and that, in fact, I was still very emotionally tied to the dance world. The way I initially got back into it was through my private practice. I was seeing a number of patients who had been dancers, as well as other people in the related fields of music and art and I started to formulate ways of connecting the two worlds of dance and medicine. Also, I began collaborating with Marian Horosko on a series of articles for *Dance Magazine* called 'Stress and the Dancer,' which dealt with issues relating to everyone from the young student to the retired performer. Since there is a very delicate interface between art and science, I felt that I had the ideal opportunity to do something more for dancers.

In the last few years, what's come to fruition is a combination of the two. A special clinic called PACH (Performing Arts Center for Health) with a psychiatric department has been set up at Bellevue Hospital. The clinic grew from an idea. A small group of professionals gathered together and developed a vision of a comprehensive health center for people in the performing arts. Because these people have some very special characteristics and needs, their health care should be something special too. The injured dancer usually has to see an orthopedist and a radiologist. At some point he or she may want to see a nutritionist. We see a lot of complex problems with eating, both overeating and undereating, and so nutrition is an important element. I became involved through their need for a psychiatric component.

I have discovered through the years that the effect of stress is probably the most important factor which determines whether a dancer succeeds or not: how the dancer handles the stress of performing, coming to a new city, joining a company, dealing with family pressures, meeting people, and making friends. There's so much involved that I feel the psychiatric component is very important. While psychiatrists generally are very sensitive to the special needs of certain people and can understand the creativity in the performing arts, I think that seminars and some special sessions with them will be necessary and helpful in making this kind of a clinic effective. Basically, what we are doing in my division at PACH is interviewing, evaluating, and assessing anyone who has a connection with any of the performing arts. We evaluate their psychological status and help them if they have some kind of problem.

I see that a lot of the stresses that I experienced still exist, but there are some differences. Although the ballet world was competitive twenty years ago, it's a lot more competitive now. Today, many young dancers are being turned away from the top schools and companies because they don't have an ideal body. Twenty years ago, auditions were infrequent. Now, auditions, competitions, prizes, trophies, and awards for scholarships are widespread. This makes it a lot more stressful for young people today. Dancers are very technically proficient and very concerned about technique. While that may also have been true twenty years ago, I think the technical standard is now a lot higher and so are the expectations. I don't know that the motivation is really that much different today than it was, and to put it simply, I think that most young dancers love to dance.

Common patterns of behavior seem to evolve for dancers in transition, though that may be true for people in any kind of career transition. There are questions, doubts, past experiences, and elements in each person's background that play a significant role. But one of the problems I've noticed that is more common to dancers is the self-doubt they experience in being able to pursue another career. They also have a type of identity crisis. Without an identity as a dancer, it takes a while to develop enough of a sense of self and ego strength to successfully move on to something else. That's not as common in other career transitions as it is in dancer transitions. Yet one of the biggest assets of dancers is the discipline they had during their years of working, and that discipline can be utilized in whatever career they choose. Of course, during the period of transition there can be so many doubts that sometimes even their biggest asset fails them.

Personal experience will determine the direction one takes in a second career. In other words, if there has been family support for academic pursuit, or for a particular career, this may have an influence on the dancer in transition. Also, the individual's special talents are important.

I think injuries today are more frequently a cause for career transition. There is a greater degree of injury-related early retirement and that may be due to the increased technical demands that are now made on dancers. Of course, career transition still exists for the person who stops due to aging, or what I call premature aging. In fact, these people are in their mid-thirties and their forties and, although that may not sound exactly aged, it is for a dancer. The difference in age-related retirement between this generation of dancers and the previous one is that dancers lasted a lot longer than they do now. Careers today are quite brief in comparison. The average length of stay in a professional ballet company is a lot shorter now. The frustration level, the impulse control, the dissatisfaction, all of these seem to peak a lot sooner than they did in the past.

There are a lot of socio-cultural differences in this generation. I think that any issue we address is more clearly understood if we take these into account. The pressures on young people today are different from those of the previous generation. It also seems as if young dancers now have a much better sense of their value and work as performers. In fact it has almost reached the point of over-confidence. Their expectations of what the performing world is going to do for them, rather than what they're going to contribute to that world, is very different. They expect a lot and are not prepared to make the kinds of sacrifices that dancers of a generation ago made. The kind of acceptance that dancers now have encourages them, and there is not so much of a stigma about being a dancer. A generation ago, you didn't know what to expect, so you didn't expect very much.

I would like to see some preparation for transition with younger dancers, but one of the biggest problems is that to discuss the future with a young dancer is a very difficult matter. Most dancers are very strong-willed and don't want to think about the future; they don't want to talk about retirement, pensions, other resources, or developing other talents. In fact, they are frequently encouraged to concentrate solely on their dancing, which makes sense now in terms of their performance but really does not prepare them for the future and what might become necessary later.

The ability to go ahead, to do something else and to do it successfully, may stem from that sense of security or confidence you get when someone you respect thinks highly of you. But the period of transition is still not an easy time. Unless dancers have matured enough to establish their own family or their own set of friends, the loss of the ballet or dance company has a profound effect, because not only are they losing their identity as a dancer, they are losing a crucial support system.

There is life after dance! If we want young dancers to mature and become healthy adults, they have to think about such things. If such thinking is discouraged by people around them, there's no reason for them to face it. If it is encouraged and given a more positive profile, it can only be of benefit to the individual."

# ANGELA LEIGH

*"During transition, dancers need to have patience, courage, and a time of retreat from the daily conditions of their tightly structured lives as performers. It's a very difficult thing to realize that one is creating one's own life. I think one must try to make life the art."*

*Photograph by Ken Bell*

*Photograph by Jim Forte with permission from Angela Leigh*

*Angela was born in Kampala, East Africa. The family moved to London, England, when she was six, and her ballet studies began there with Lydia Kyasht. At fourteen she was accepted at the Sadler's Wells School (later the Royal Ballet School) and studied there for two years. At sixteen she performed and toured with a London Palladium show. After a year, she left the show, got married, and moved with her husband to Canada, where she established successful dance schools in Orillia and Barrie, Ontario. Their daughter Stephanie was born in 1949 in Orillia.*

*Angela joined the National Ballet of Canada when it was founded in 1951. During her fifteen years with the company, she became a principal dancer and danced most of the leading classical and contemporary roles. She also spent a year as guest artist with England's Western Theatre Ballet, touring southern England and appearing in their London season.*

*Retiring as a dancer in 1966, she went on to teach and choreograph at the National Ballet School, the National Ballet of Canada, George Brown College, and the Dance Department at York University, where she was an assistant professor for four years. She has also applied her creativity to the field of fabric art, producing works which range from framed art and wall hangings to designer fabrics for interiors. Since 1977, her creations, under the name Mantra Design, have been exhibited in galleries, mainly in the Toronto area. An artist and interior designer, Angela still maintains her involvement with dance through her teaching at York University and George Brown College.*

"First of all, I think dancers have to start listening to themselves. The way I reached my current art form was by going back to my childhood and re-discovering former gifts, talents, and interests. The first one, dance, has been with me since I can remember. We all have undiscovered gifts, and, instead of rushing around getting anxious about what the next step is going to be after a life of dancing, one should take a step back and listen to the internal record of one's life. A dancer can find that his or her whole motivation for life is gone when the dancing ends, because suddenly there is this great empty space. In fact, it isn't empty at all. It just has to be nurtured. You have to start spending time with yourself, and when you start to listen to yourself your intuition will be your guide. You have to trust that guidance and realize that when one destiny is fulfilled it's time to move on to the next one.

I started to study ballet at six with Lydia Kyasht after my family moved to London from East Africa. She was a divine teacher, a very encouraging, warm, wonderful woman, and she inspired me. Without that kind of inspiration I would never have stayed with it. I can remember the audition I did for her. It was in a studio with balconies at either end. I was six and I had always danced on my toes. She was sitting with Nicolas Legat and they both watched while I did my little dance. The first thing Kyasht said to my mother was, 'We're going to have to take her off her toes!' After a while Kyasht started giving me extra classes. I guess she thought I had something. I saw her years later, just before I joined the National Ballet of Canada, and she was still teaching. I was twenty at the time and I said to her, 'Do you think I'm too old to dance?' She said, 'Too old! I'm nearly seventy-five and I'm still dancing!' So I thought, okay, if you can do it, so can I!

Another great inspiration was Margot Fonteyn, who used to take Saturday classes with Kyasht. She was about sixteen at the time, and I will always remember the times I stood behind her at the barre. I left Kyasht at age ten because my parents wanted me to go to boarding school in southern England. That lasted until I was fourteen, and then I returned to London and auditioned for the Sadler's Wells School (now the Royal Ballet School). After the audition, I remember going into Ninette de Valois' office, where she told my mother that I had a tendency towards flat feet and that I had to be guided out of that one!

It was during the war when I started there, and I used to carry a gas mask to classes because of the possibility that we might have to go down into the air raid shelter underneath. Nicolai Sergeyev was teaching and his classes were absolutely wonderful. Another teacher I remember well was Ailne Phillips. She used to sit on a chair and move her hands around and chant 'glissade assemblé,' but she never got off the chair to move around and I found that tricky. There were also times when Vera Volkova came and taught and, occasionally, de Valois would come and give a class. All this in London between bombs!

While I was at the Sadler's Wells School, the company would come in and rehearse. With people like Pamela May, June Brae, Michael Somes, Leslie Edwards, and Robert Helpmann rehearsing, it was exciting, but I got fed up when I was about sixteen and decided it was all going a bit slow. Can you imagine? At sixteen! Anyway, I went to an audition at the Palladium for a new musical called *Strike It Again*. I didn't know anything about auditions. I didn't know you were supposed to plan what you were going to do and to bring your own music. I arrived in the dressing room and everyone else there was in costume, getting ready, and there I was not knowing what was going to happen! All the people were going on stage, doing their solos and 'Thank you very much' and all that. Then, it was my turn and I got onto the stage and the choreographer, Wendy Toye, said, What are you going to do?' I said, 'I don't know.' 'Well, didn't you bring any music?' 'No.' Finally, I just improvised to a waltz that the pianist was kind enough to play because I didn't know what else to do! I remember being lined up and chosen as one of eight to go out with this musical. And that was why I left the Sadler's Wells School. We went to Blackpool and the production worked out rather well. It was brought back to London and was a success. I stayed about a year with the show and then decided to leave and get married to a Canadian, Clayton Leigh.

The following year, my husband and I came to Canada. I thought I was going to be the wife with the apron in a little cottage! I also knew I wanted to dance, but there was nothing going on in Canada at that time. We went to Ottawa first and then, after about a year, moved to Orillia where I started a school. (Later, I started another school in Barrie.) It was at this time, in 1949, that my daughter Stephanie was born and she added a new dimension to my life.

In 1951 I heard about Celia Franca. She'd come over, at the invitation of a group of people in Toronto who were trying to raise money to finance a ballet company, and was teaching on Sundays at Boris Volkoff's studio. I would drive in from Orillia to take her class. I remember going up to her at the end of the very first class and saying, 'I would like to join your company.' I don't think she was quite ready for that one, since I hadn't danced in about four and a half years! But she did accept me, and so we moved to Toronto when the National Ballet company was formed in September.

Those first years with the company were divine, except that we didn't have any money. The first performance was at the Eaton Auditorium, and we did *Les Sylphides, Salome* (which Celia choreographed), and *Prince Igor*. Celia was inspiring. If she hadn't been, none of us would have lasted. She had a firm conviction that we were going somewhere. I was doing a lot of corps work and I remember thinking, 'I don't want to do *this* for very long.' I had my eye on other things all the time!

I think it was in the second year that Celia asked me to do the Prelude in *Les Sylphides*. I adored that role and that's when I started to get really serious about the whole thing. Celia was as extraordinary a coach as she was a dancer. She gave you a motivation beyond movement itself. Her coaching encompassed feeling, thinking, and a close affinity with the music. I loved working with her on a one-to-one basis. She demanded that you raise the level of your concentration, and that was the thing that made her difficult, as it was very hard to get to her level. She took the firm line that you had to seek for your best at all times. That's why I really appreciate her. Of course, we had lots of battles too during the fifteen years I was with the company.

We performed a lot of Antony Tudor's works. He came to do *Lilac Garden, Gala Performance,* and *Offenbach in the Underworld.* I remember understudying The Other Woman in *Lilac Garden* for what seemed an awfully long time. But meanwhile, I was doing The Russian Ballerina in *Gala,* my first big part for Tudor. His insights into motivation really turned the lights on for me in terms of how and why to dance. Tudor gave you incredible images. By nature I was a very lightweight dancer, and I remember that for *Gala* he gave me the image of being a giant condor, a very large creature, and got this comic Russian Ballerina out of me. That's the biggest lesson of comedy: to do it all with great seriousness, as though you're doing drama. In fact, with that kind of seriousness the laugh comes from the situation the person is in. He taught me that, and from then on I always worked from that internal point of view. An abstract work, however, was always more difficult because it was pure structure. I would 'architecturalize' it, and think of lines, forms and curves.

I think we had a connection with the audience in those days that is missing today. When the company moved to the O'Keefe Centre in Toronto I felt a great gap between myself and the audience. Performing had become far more impersonal, somehow, and mass-produced. It seems that some companies make it a priority to reach the largest number of people they can. I don't know if any art is really improved in that way.

I spent only one year away during the fifteen years I was with the National Ballet. In 1965 I went to England and was a guest artist with Western Theatre Ballet. While the company had a very good repertoire, I was glad to get back to the National after the tour because, at that time, the repertoire there was even more interesting and I was being offered some challenging roles.

My second husband, Paul Almond, was a television producer and I began to meet a lot of actors, technicians, set designers, and directors, and it all had a great influence on my work. I would listen to someone like Kate Reid talk about her roles with Paul. When they spoke of how they went about working on a scene, how they motivated it, I would try to apply that to what I was doing. Technique is in the head, and if you can figure it out in the head, somehow the body follows. For instance, if I was stuck in my body trying to develop thirty-two fouettés without a motive as to *why* I did those thirty-two fouettés I would never have been able to do them because, technically, I don't think I could have done them. But, because I was motivated to do them for a reason, I could get myself to be that character on stage to such an extent that *she* had the staying power to do those thirty-two fouettés.

We're all psychological creatures I think. If I'm doing an abstract painting, I might be thinking of line, form and color, but I know the colors can mean something psychologically. When I did Balanchine's *Concerto Barocco*, I was probably far too dramatic in my interpretation. That kind of abstract ballet has a meaning of its own. It has a psychological balance which is achieved through the timing, being one with the music, and through an understanding of the phrasing and architecture of the work.

Eventually, an end to dancing does come and, for me, there were many reasons to stop. First of all, I broke my foot and came back too soon. If I'd been intelligent I would have taken the season off, but I decided to get back as soon as I could. At the time, I also felt my range of characters was being curbed. I don't think I fully appreciated the extent of my humorous side then because comedy seemed very easy to me. I thought it was too light. Of course, comedy is really the deepest thing of all, but I didn't realize that. I just wanted a greater diversity of roles. I think that was one of the main reasons I decided to leave the company, and now I'm very glad that I left when I did. At the time I didn't like the idea, but in retrospect I think it was time for me to stop. I was ready to absorb all the information I had gained through dancing and get a little deeper into myself. If you have some intuition developed, you can realize that when a door closes on you, it's not always for a negative reason. I'm not saying that I didn't get upset about it. In fact, I thought it was a kind of death, and I couldn't cope with it at all.

I had a very difficult time at first, but I was fortunate because Betty Oliphant invited me to teach at the National Ballet School. I wasn't quite ready to see myself as a teacher, but nevertheless I did do some teaching. It wasn't something that was motivated from my depths like dancing had been. I mean, I didn't have a choice with dancing.

Teaching was more objective, more intellectual, and was very natural for me. It didn't seem to be a big transition. However, I still didn't know if that was really what I wanted to do. I wondered why I didn't have the same drive and ambition I'd had as a dancer.

I was also working in a antique shop once a week, and Frances Downing, an ex-member of the company, came by and we started to chat. She told me that she had consulted a Buddhist monk (Ananda Bodhi) who was in town. At that time, I didn't know the first thing about Buddhism, and I thought, well, this sounds interesting. She asked if I'd come to the next meeting, and I went. I sat and listened to him give a lecture. He mesmerized me! I continued going to his lectures and discovered that his whole approach to life and what one should be aiming for were diametrically opposed to what I'd been doing. Because of the discontent I was feeling, I began to accept this new way of thinking.

The Buddhist philosophy was far from anything I'd known spiritually through Christianity and my Church of England upbringing. The whole idea was so poetic and the imagery so incredible! I was exploring feelings that I'd probably always had as a dancer, but which I hadn't previously been able to intellectualize. I began to understand that all the work I'd done as a dancer had been spiritual, not physical. I realized that I'd been expressing many of the Buddhist laws through the imagery and motivation of what I'd been doing. I started to study Buddhist teachings, and I went to India for a while to continue my studies.

When I returned from India in 1968, Betty Oliphant asked me to teach again, and I did. Being the kind of person she is and very understanding of the transition I was going through, she allowed me to put in a program of yoga at the beginning of my classes. I also did quite a lot of choreography at the school, and I produced an evening of my own works. I taught at the school for two years.

I continued to study Buddhist teachings with Ananda Bodhi, and I noticed that some people were going to his basement after the meetings. He was teaching them to batik. I went to a couple of sessions, found batiking most interesting and, before I knew it, I had this gigantic work table in my basement.

While I was teaching at the National Ballet School, there was a wonderful art teacher there, Pat Goss. In between my classes, I'd go upstairs to the art studio and start working on a few batiks. Then I thought that perhaps I would do that instead of teaching. However,

113

Grant Strate was starting a dance department at York University, and he asked me to teach there. I thought this was very exciting, and so I agreed. While I was teaching at York with students of all shapes and sizes, both trained and untrained, I was also asked to give company class for the National Ballet. There was quite a difference between the company with all its perfection and York, where the program was clearly experimental. It was a fascinating time. And in the middle of all this I started choreographing and staging shows! I did a review called *Oh, Coward!* Then I did *Hey, Porter!*, a Cole Porter anthology, *Gilbert & Sullivan Tonight!* and *Noel and Gertie*, which I directed as well as staged.

Eventually, however, I decided to start my own design consulting business. I didn't know the first thing about business: how to run a company, do books, advertize and sell my product. It became necessary to learn all those things. But, that's been the fascination — doing it on my own. The main thing I learned from Ananda Bodhi was to be able to motivate myself and stand on my own two feet. During the course of my dancing career, I'd been standing on my own two feet all right, but I hadn't known how an audience turned up in front of me, who paid the electricians to light me, how that set got behind me, and so on. Now I have a greater understanding of how things in my life work because I've had to do them all myself. This teaches you great independence if you can survive, and, luckily, through dancing, I learned how to survive. One of the things I realized was that everything that happens to you is totally your own doing, and *that* knowledge is very important.

I named my company Mantra, which is a Sanskrit word. In Western terms, mantra is an affirmation, like, 'I love all things and all things love me.' It's also an organization of words, a design of words. When I design someone's room I'm working on an affirmation. In fact, I'm making that affirmation visual. All the symbols I use in my work relate to the inner visual world, which is different from the external one. It works like a *mandala*, which is a circle used in meditation; you pinpoint the center, and that centers your whole self.

My work has involved a lot of experimentation. I've worked with every fabric I can think of that's a natural fiber and each one has its own life. Once you've established the type of fabric for a design project, you can start to get into the style the client wants. Usually, I've been very fortunate in the people with whom I've worked as they have more or less given me carte blanche.

114

In my work I'm always alternating. It's just like dancing a varied repertoire. I like variety, and I like having to deal with the raw materials all the time. In a way it's like using your body. You're stuck with your body, whether you like it or not, and you have to work your way through that to do different roles. In my work it's the same sort of principle. I enjoy creating the fabric even more than what I make with it, and I always have to keep in mind where the fabric is going. If it's going to be a painting or a hanging, I have total freedom. I'm exploring quilting now, and I'm becoming very three-dimensional on that level. It's more like soft sculpture. When it comes to the more practical things, like cushions, bedspreads, blinds, or drapes, I go into somebody's home and co-ordinate with the colors that are already in the room. I love that!

What I'm mainly doing now is consulting. I go out and visit a person's home and then consult with them about what they want to do with a room. If I'm using the inner levels of knowledge that I've acquired, it eventually has to come through that I'm using those inner symbols on the cloth. Studying the mind and how it works has been my greatest obsession. Everybody in the dance world thought we were in our bodies. We weren't. We were in our minds! Nothing is created except through the mind, and color is all emotion.

I find that expression through fabric work gives me a lifestyle I like, one I can manage. I have a great deal of freedom to decide what I'm going to do and when I'm going to do it. I'm not saying that this freedom is easily won. You do have to go through the whole financial battle of life. You have to pay your rent, your bills, buy food, all that sort of thing. At the same time, you try to create a lifestyle. I think this is what I have discovered, that the basic thing is to get a lifestyle that suits you, to find your own rhythm and work with it. The nature of the work hasn't changed, just the rhythm of it. I also like the independence I have now.

Dancers are not one-sided people. If they are gifted as dancers, they tend to be gifted in many other areas. Many dancers have imagination and the ability to create. If they have used their time well as dancers, if they have tried to be creative and not let other people tell them everything, they are going to grow in whatever field they choose. There are so many other forms that their creativity can take. One does have to have patience, though, to find out what those other gifts are. During transition, dancers need to have patience, courage, and a time of retreat from the daily conditions of their tightly structured lives as performers. It's a very difficult thing to realize that one is creating one's own life. I think one must try to make life the art."

# SAM MOSES

*"I think many people continue dancing because it's the only thing they know and they don't want to make a transition. But it's one of those hurdles that, as a human being, you have to go through. Basically, I'm grateful for having had a focus for that length of time. There was something to attain every day. It was a clear, clear focus and I knew what I wanted. I'm grateful for that. It has influenced every part of my life since."*

Photograph by Courtney McMahon

*Photograph by Anne Moses*

## EXCHANGES: LIFE AFTER DANCE

*Sam was born in Bangalore, India, and when he was ten moved with his family to Vancouver, where he studied dance with Kay Armstrong. At seventeen, he was invited by Betty Oliphant to study at the National Ballet School in Toronto. After graduating, he went on to dance with the National Ballet of Canada from 1962 to 1966. He did his first work for television in National Ballet productions of* The Nutcracker *and* Romeo and Juliet. *Sam left the National Ballet to work extensively as a dancer/singer for television and film. His first experience as an actor was in* Spring Thaw *at the Royal Alexandra Theatre in Toronto. He was immediately invited to join the Shaw Festival company and later the Stratford Festival, where he was awarded the prestigious Tyrone Guthrie Award for his performance in* Life in Paris.

*Sam has had major acting and singing roles in many plays and musicals such as* Godspell, Fiddler on the Roof, The Fantastiks, Guys and Dolls, A Man for all Seasons, Twelfth Night, Bent, *and* School for Wives. *His film work includes* Moscow on the Hudson *and* Ghost Busters *and he has many radio and television commercial credits. Sam and his wife Anne have two children and now live in Toronto.*

"For me, dance started with sports — track and field in school. I was breaking all kinds of records in high jumping, broad jumping and everything else. Once, I watched *The Nutcracker* on television and, turning to my sister who loved dancing, said, 'That isn't as difficult as sports.' She said, on a dare, 'Why don't you try it?' So I did! I went to Kay Armstrong's Ballet School in Vancouver. I had a working scholarship and, surprisingly, my sister was right; I found that it was, indeed, more difficult than sports. It also helped my sports a great deal.

After I had trained intensively for two years, Betty Oliphant from the National Ballet School came to Vancouver for our Cecchetti ballet examinations. She must have seen potential in me, because I was offered a full scholarship to the National Ballet School. I was grateful. Later, I realized how much! At seventeen I wasn't doing very well academically and at that time had no idea of a vocation, so I was quite happy and excited to go to Toronto. Being the last of eleven children and somewhat spoiled, I was afraid to think of how very lonely it might be away from home. I decided not to think about that, because had I wanted to I could have scared myself into not going.

Eventually I graduated from the ballet school and was asked by Celia Franca to join the National Ballet of Canada. I really enjoyed it at the beginning. I was doing something I loved and was being paid for

120

it, but it began to dawn on me that, because ballet was such a pure art form, it might have limitations for me in terms of self-expression. I also felt I was young enough to leave and still go back if I ever wanted to. As time went on, I became unhappy in the company. I disliked being in the corps because I couldn't stand doing what everyone else did. It was extremely restricting, but I worked very, very hard and eventually was given some really nice roles in pieces like *One in Five* (choreographed by Ray Powell), which I loved because of the dramatic and humorous qualities it required and because you were able to communicate something. You tend to embrace the challenges more in a ballet like that. This was what I was looking for! Unfortunately, at that time, there wasn't enough of that kind of fulfillment, so I decided to leave. I kept up with my dance training and moved into the medium of television.

I knew television was an option because we had done *Nutcracker* and *Romeo and Juliet* for television, and I felt that I could work in this field. It was surprisingly easy because of my dance training, which was used to great advantage in television shows. I did CBC's *Tommy Hunter Show* and *The Good Company*, CFTO's *The Pig and Whistle*, and some specials. It may be difficult for others to understand the dilemma faced by those who first make a decision to go into dance and who then realize that perhaps physically or psychologically they may have made the wrong decision. The usual alternative is to teach, which is fine if you want to go in that direction.

I knew I could sing, and so it seemed natural to move into musicals. I auditioned for *Spring Thaw*, a musical revue directed by Paxton Whitehead, and was hired for this production at the Royal Alexandra Theatre in Toronto. It was my first opportunity to express myself as an actor, singer, and dancer. Something clicked! Although I felt I was moving in the right direction, I also found it somewhat terrifying. After the show closed, Paxton invited me to do the Shaw Festival. In retrospect, I think I must have been dreadful! I hadn't realized the strength and simplicity of the spoken word. I was still thinking in terms of being a dancer. As a dancer in the corps, you're programmed to imitate a series of movements without subtext. Acting demands that you create that subtext, and I didn't know about that yet.

Around that time, I married Anne Steele, also a former dancer with the National Ballet. Financially, we were comparatively well-off then, as both Anne and I were doing very well in television shows. We were making more than in the corps at the National, but somehow it wasn't the same. There was so much more that we appreciated about ballet and we began to realize the nature of the compromises involved. I was going through a re-training period. I knew in the back of my mind that acting was what I wanted. It's been only in the last six years that I've understood why. Perhaps with the knowledge that I now have of what acting is about, I can see that I may have been able to apply myself to dance in the same way.

The next step was children's theatre in Vancouver, at the Holiday Playhouse. The work was great and it lasted two years. Steady work meant I could enjoy the luxury of having a family. Our first son, Karim David, was born — funny that I should be doing children's theatre at the time! During the second year I auditioned for Stratford and was accepted into the company. Another long run and another child! Ari, our second son, was born.

At Stratford, I was Jack Creley's understudy in *Life in Paris*. We did a performance for Stratford Festival Director, Jean Gascon, who was quite impressed with my work, and that year I received the Tyrone Guthrie Award. After Stratford, I went to Theatre London and did *The Fantastiks* and *School for Wives* for Jean Gascon. Then I traveled to Winnipeg for *Fiddler on the Roof* and *Godspell*, and a lot of other shows before heading out to Theatre New Brunswick where I acted mostly in musicals, and a cabaret show called *Flicks*, which ran for about a year and a half. During that time, I was able to relax with the knowledge of a certain security and continuity in my life, and was able to take a closer look at myself as an actor. Although I enjoyed the cabaret show I was doing, I did feel that it lacked a certain kind of perspective. I started studying with Kurt Reis at CAST (Centre for Actor's Study in Toronto), and what he was saying seemed to answer the questions I was asking. It became extremely exciting because what he said, basically, was that you work from yourself, from your own experience of life. It seemed to me that this meant that the more you understood life, the more you had to offer your art. Life complements art — they grow with each other. I was moving into the realm of representational theatre.

A confusion emerged. As a dancer, and so far as an actor, I had been trying to be someone other than myself, and now I was discovering that acting demanded that I be myself totally. I had wanted to be an actor because I didn't want to be myself — at least not a dancer! I began to realize, however, that when you become someone else you immediately limit yourself because you start to think about what this person is doing, instead of just being there and letting it come out of you. I began to discover the extent of the resources within myself. You have to work with an understanding that what you are doing is still learning. Technique, and this is my interpretation, is what you use when you don't understand something instinctively. If you can do it instinctively, don't worry about why or how — just do it. However, if you start thinking of doing it in terms of being judged, or where your next work is, you're dead from the beginning.

As an actor and in terms of art, I felt limited in Toronto. Theatre is international, and we must do it everywhere because the language of thought is universal. For me, New York was the gateway. When I went to New York I felt the possibilities were enormous. Ideally, I would like to be able to live and work wherever I want, keeping Toronto as my home. But at one point New York was beckoning because things were going well there. I did some movies, including one for Paul Mazursky — a lovely scene with Robin Williams in *Moscow on the Hudson*, and another for Columbia Pictures, *Ghost Busters*, with Dan Ackroyd and Bill Murray.

I have two teenage boys, and living in two places has its complications. You can't help feeling that you're missing out on something and you deal with it the best way you can. Basically, I go where the work is. It can be very lonely in New York, but having a secure family life here in Toronto provides a very strong base from which to step out. Right now I'm doing *A Chorus Line* here in Toronto and loving it. Next, who knows?

My ambition is to be able to say no to the things I don't want to do and to find roles that say something that I would like to say. I don't really care about stardom, except that it offers you that ability to say no. I feel I've done my groundwork and I feel now that I am quite prepared to handle whatever comes, knowing that this is what I want to do. My experience as a dancer gave me an understanding of the physical. The discipline that goes with dance, what you have to achieve and how rewarding it can be — it's all there for you to examine and use. The journey is the gift! I would do it again, being a dancer, because its demands gave me a direction. It's very difficult to leave because you work so hard to achieve it. I think many people continue dancing because it's the only thing they know and they don't want to make a transition. But it's one of those hurdles that, as a human being, you have to go through. Basically, I'm grateful for having had a focus for that length of time. There was something to attain every day. It was a clear, clear focus and I knew what I wanted. I'm grateful for that. It has influenced every part of my life since."

# ANDREW OXENHAM

*"I think today a lot of people play at being dancers. They want to be good dancers and they push themselves to be technically good, but they just don't have that spark that makes them an involved dancer, that extra measure of commitment that makes them an artist."*

*Photograph by Anthony Crickmay*

126

Photograph by Rolf Kalman, from Dance Today in Canada published by Simon & Pierre, Toronto.

127

*Andrew was born in London, England. He began dance classes at age seven at the Bristol School of Dancing, home of Western Theatre Ballet, and made his first stage appearance with them at age ten. Andrew's family migrated to Canada in 1957, and he continued his dance studies with Gweneth Lloyd in Toronto. He then entered the National Ballet School in 1960, graduating in 1964, the first boy to graduate from that school.*

*Andrew joined the National Ballet of Canada in 1964 and became a soloist in 1966. He took a three-year leave of absence from 1970 to 1973 to dance with John Cranko's company in Stuttgart, West Germany, becoming a soloist with that company in 1972. He returned to Canada and the National Ballet in 1973, but after a year decided to retire from dancing as a result of a chronic back injury. In 1975 he married Kathleen Trick, also a former National Ballet dancer, and began a new career in dance and theatre photography.*

*He is now an official photographer for the National Ballet of Canada and has many photographic commitments to other Canadian dance and theatre companies. He is the author of two books —* Dance Today in Canada *(Toronto: Simon and Pierre, 1977) and* Puppetry in Canada *(Toronto: Ontario Puppetry Association, 1980) — and is currently preparing a book on the National Ballet of Canada. Andrew and Kathleen live in Pickering, Ontario, and have two children, Oliver and Emily.*

"I was born in London, England, and later moved to Bristol, where my sister studied dance at the school of Western Theatre Ballet. My mother didn't have a babysitter so I went along and took classes too. Eventually my sister quit and I kept going. I think I was too young to know what it was all about. It was fun and yet it was horrible because at that time dancing was not considered a suitable profession for a man. We went to public school and my dance classes were at an awkward time, but it was rewarding overall. I knew then that I wanted to be a dancer even though I used to get into a lot of fights about it.

My family and I came to Canada in 1957. I studied with Gweneth Lloyd for three years until I went to the National Ballet School in Toronto. In those days there were only thirty people at the school, so we all had our own private audition. That first year at the school there were only Howard Marcus and I as full-time male students, with twenty-eight girls. I was the first boy to graduate from the National Ballet School, and while I was doing my post-graduate year there was a vacancy in the company and they asked me to join.

It was my nineteenth birthday when I signed the contract — my first contract! But I found life in the company miserable. I'd been at

128

the school when there were only thirty students. We were a small group of dancers working with a small number of teachers, so when we finally got out into the big, bad world, it was a shock because we suddenly discovered that we were not as special as we thought we were.

I think I was going through a transition of relating to the real world when I left the company on a leave of absence for three years in 1970. I wanted to broaden my experiences because (and I'm sure many people have the same experience) when you are in one environment for a long time you tend to stagnate and the people that see you every day stagnate. You end up just doing the same parts over and over again. So I went to Stuttgart. At that time, many dancers at the National Ballet wanted to go to Germany to work with John Cranko's company, because when he did *Romeo and Juliet* for the National it had a tremendous impact on everyone. Suddenly there was this whole different world of movement available to us, not just endless fifth positions in classical ballets. You had to get out there on stage and try to be a human being and you had to act. If you were a peasant in the corps de ballet, you had to *be* a peasant. There wasn't any standing around and looking beautiful — you had to be an integral part of the story.

I continued to have difficulties in the Stuttgart Company, however. I discovered one of the troublesome things in life as a dancer and a performer: if your career doesn't allow you to develop as a person, which is what I feel happened in my case, you don't turn out to be the type of dancer that you envision. I took too long to grow up. Not physically though. Physically I was very capable of doing it all. My Stuttgart experience made me see that I wasn't going to be the same sort of person for the rest of my life. I was changing, developing, and growing mentally, all because of the atmosphere of the Stuttgart Company.

Cranko influenced me. He changed the shape of my life. He taught me how to think and gave me insight into the process of being objective about myself. He showed me the many dimensions of human beings. I also learned by seeing the way his dancers applied themselves to their performances. Cranko used to do two or three new ballets a year, and it was a creative process that really involved us. I had finally been made a soloist in 1973. It was a bit anticlimactic in the way it happened, because when I first got to Stuttgart I was in the Opera Ballet. I'd assumed all the leads in that company and I didn't

129

have so much as a day off for a year. I wasn't meant to be in the big company, but eventually I was, and I got more and more roles and was actually a soloist the year before they made me one. At that point I was happy and had a very satisfying career. On the other hand I didn't like living in Germany at all.

Finally, I decided to return to Canada, knowing that I would stop dancing in a short time because I didn't want to go on. When I came back to the National Ballet I got the same parts as I'd had when I left, and I decided not to continue. Also, I'd had a back injury which had been going on for quite a while and it was going into my feet. It got to the point where I couldn't stand in first position in the morning and I used to get thoroughly discouraged and bad-tempered. I kept going to the doctor and it didn't get better. All these factors contributed to my decision to leave the company. I had been thinking about it for a long time — many years. When was I going to give it up? Why was I giving it up? There were many possible answers. One had to do with the career itself. I thought about alternatives and decided not to teach. I wouldn't have the patience for it since I hate doing the same thing day after day.

I think today a lot of people play at being dancers. They want to be good dancers and they push themselves to be technically good, but they just don't have that spark that makes them an involved dancer, that extra measure of commitment that makes them an artist. I don't think those qualities can be developed. They're instinctive. You can bring them out as Cranko did, but they have to be there in the first place. I thought that perhaps I did not have that extra quality and I also saw that I didn't want to continue with the same old parts, not getting any better or any worse. That was one reason why I gave up dancing. It was around this time that I met my wife Kathleen, who was also a dancer with the company. It was the first time I'd ever wanted to get that involved and get married.

I had been doing a little photography on and off through the years, but I hadn't really done anything serious. I just took pictures and developed them, made prints for the dancers, that sort of thing. I think I had a lot of nerve because I didn't know anything about photography at that time. I took all my pictures and I started going around to people. I worked on a project about how a ballet was put together. I took it to various publishers and that's how my book *Dance Today in Canada* came about. I went to one publisher and he said, 'Okay, we've been meaning to do a book on dance in Canada, so why don't you go about getting a Canada Council grant to do it?' I applied for a grant and on the second try was successful. I learned through the continuous process of taking photographs and looking at them, analyzing them, talking to other photographers, and just being aware of what I was doing.

I worked for a while as an assistant for a photographer, Anthony Crickmay, who used to photograph the National Ballet. We did all the darkroom and lighting work together, and I learned most of what I now know from him. When I did the book, everything was photographed from dead center, so that's why a lot of the pictures look very flat. I wanted to show dancers from an audience's point of view, and at that time I was better at doing the more intimate moments of dance, because these were a little slower and easier to capture on camera.

I think my vision of photography has evolved because now it's a challenging job. When I was doing the book, it wasn't so much of a job. Now I have to produce a number of photographs in, say, an hour. You've got an hour with all these dancers coming in and running around, and you have to be very calm and collected while going about doing your job. One thing I do feel about it — you have to make dancers look like people. You have to make them look as beautiful or expressive as you can, but you have to present them as people, not as sterile objects, not as the things you see fifty feet away on the stage. You have to try and make them look involved within the context of what they're doing. Maybe I'm trying to draw something out of them as a photographer that I couldn't draw out of myself as a dancer. On the other hand, I use all the science and technology that I can to enhance my work.

I have grown from what I was to what I am now, and I want to keep evolving as a person and a photographer. I feel I have a control in the medium of photography that I didn't have as a dancer. My present life evolves in many ways — the same publisher who published the dance book was putting together a book on puppetry. I was the logical choice for the book because we had previously worked together and they wanted quite a theatrical-looking book — they wanted the puppets to have a sense of movement. The book was published in 1980, and I'm quite pleased with it.

I also do house renovations. When you are a poor, starving artist, you have to find cheap houses to fix up. We bought two cheap houses — we lived in one for four years, fixed it up, and sold it. We bought another one recently and it was the junk house of the street — walls falling down, a total mess. We fixed that one up too, and one day we'll sell that and buy another. I taught myself to do house renovations in the same way that I learned photography — by being observant. One of the things I'm grateful for is that the National Ballet School taught me how to teach myself. If you're intelligent and you've been taught in such a way that you are open, you can do anything you want to do.

I find that I work harder now as a photographer than I did as a dancer. It's mentally more exhausting because as a photographer I'm a one-man show. I have to do it all and there is only one chance to do it properly. If I weren't disciplined, I couldn't do it. That form of discipline is very good and is an aid to being creative because you don't waste time doing things unnecessarily. If you are independent you have to have a certain logic which takes you towards that independence. You guide the energy to the result. It's a question of having the confidence to transfer that energy to a new area."

# MARCOS PAREDES

*"I need to keep growing. The world of performing is a continuous growing process. Every single night, every performance we give, is an opportunity to grow. Even if we do the same ballet fifty times, we cannot do it the same way. That process has to translate into life."*

133

**MARCOS PAREDES**

HILARION IN GISELLE

*Photograph by Kenn Duncan*

134

*Photograph by Bil Leidersdorf*

## EXCHANGES: LIFE AFTER DANCE

*Marcos was born in the city of Aguascalientes, Mexico. He studied painting, drawing, sculpture, and architectural drawing at the regional school of the Fine Arts Institute, Mexico City, and later became interested in ballet through watching the classes his sister took there. When he was thirteen, arrangements were made for him to study ballet privately as boys were not permitted to join the girls at class. At fifteen, he was awarded a scholarship to the National School in Mexico City and continued his academic and dance studies there. During his four years at the National School, Marcos first joined the Ballet Contemporaneo in Mexico City. He danced with them for two years and, when he was seventeen, joined the Ballet de Camara, also for two years. Following the incorporation of these two companies to form the Ballet Classico de Mexico, he danced with the new company for a further two years.*

*In 1963 and 1964, Marcos was invited to perform as guest artist with the Denver City Ballet, and following those seasons traveled to New York where he took classes at American Ballet Theatre. He successfully auditioned for ABT and joined the company in December 1964. He danced with them for fourteen years, becoming a soloist and later principal dancer.*

*While with the company, Marcos continued to study painting and began to restore art works. When he decided to leave the company in 1979, he already had a second career in art restoration. Marcos has also designed costumes for American Ballet Theatre, the San Francisco Ballet, the Royal Winnipeg Ballet, the Ballet of Caracas, the Delta Festival Ballet of New Orleans, and the North Carolina School of the Arts. He has recently done some ballet teaching and coaching.*

"When we were children in Aguascalientes, Mexico, my mother wanted to make artists out of my eldest sister and me. She had wanted to be in the music world, but her parents would not allow it. She took us to the Academy of Art, a state-supported school and part of the Fine Arts Institute in Mexico City, where they taught dance, opera, acting, painting, and sculpture.

I was only nine, but my mother took me to all the art courses. I was learning painting, oils, sculpture, drawing, and architectural drawing. My sister was in the music branch, but she also went to the ballet school. Little by little I started to become interested in ballet. The painting room was on the second floor of an old remodeled convent, and we used to have our easels by a window looking down to the room where ballet classes were going on. Our teacher didn't want us to paint with artificial light, and one day, when it was cloudy and we had been told to put our things away and go home, I ran to the dance room where there was a class going on and stayed watching through the

136

keyhole for hours. From then on, I welcomed cloudy days! After about three years of wondering and watching I had become really fascinated. I wanted to study ballet and, since boys were not permitted to take classes with the girls, special arrangements were made for me to study privately.

At fifteen I got a scholarship to the National School in Mexico City. Our academic school training would finish at 3 o'clock and dance classes would start at 4:30. We studied ballet, modern, and Mexican folkloric dances. At night it was theory of music, languages, mime, acting, history of Mexican and universal culture, and history of dance. You can imagine this poor, provincial boy coming to class with ballet shoes, socks, a bathing suit, and a T-shirt! I was very embarrassed at first.

I never really planned what I was going to do with myself as a career. I just followed what I wanted to do. First of all, I knew that I loved the theatre. This world of make-believe, scenery, sweat, and portraying other people — that essentially is what I liked. My love for sculpture and painting gave me a sense of aesthetics. My favorite marriage of aesthetics in the theatre is in ballet or theatrical dancing of some kind, because there's sculpture in the movement. Basically, it was the love of the theatre that brought me to the ballet world. I never planned to make a career only as a dancer, but rather as an artist who would be involved in all the arts and use the dance to portray emotions — as a way of acting.

Dancers don't talk as actors do, so we are thought of as things that move and look pretty. It's up to dancers to either stay in that category of pretty, moving things or become artists. Every movement we do in our lives that is beyond walking, I think is dance. Of course, painting was always with me and I loved music. Dancing was one more aspect of art which I loved to cultivate.

During the time I was at school in Mexico City I was already dancing in a company, the Ballet Contemporaneo. After two years at the National School on a state scholarship, the director had told me, 'Marcos, I know that your government, your state, wants you to come back and become a teacher; that's why they have this scholarship for you. Would you like to be a teacher for the rest of your life?' I said, 'Of course not, I want to dance, and I want to perform as long as I can.' So he said, 'I'm going to write a letter, because I'm supposed to send the results of your accomplishments each month in order for you to keep your scholarship. I'm going to say in this letter that you have failed in many of the classes, that you have not qualified, so that they will cut your government scholarship. Then we'll keep you on here.' He sent this letter to the government of my home town! Of course, my family knew the truth and I told them not to say a word about it. I then got a National School scholarship and after two years I passed my exams.

I stayed with the Ballet Contemporaneo for two years and then decided I didn't want to continue as a modern dancer. I was seventeen at the time and I left the company, saved my money, and joined a new ballet company called Ballet de Camara in Mexico City. That company was eventually run by the state, so we had better salaries, more opportunities to perform, and longer seasons. We performed in the Palace of Fine Arts, which is the opera house. Everything suddenly came up roses in a matter of a year. In 1963 the Artistic Director of the Denver City Ballet, Averna Rose Gagnon, was in Mexico City and saw our season. She talked to the directors of the company, asking if it would be possible for me to come after our season to be a guest in their company. It was arranged and I went to Denver. It was the first time I ever saw snow in my life and my first experience with speaking English. With the money they paid me I came to New York, stayed with friends, and took classes at American Ballet Theatre. However, the money soon ran out and I had to go back to Mexico. The experience meant a lot to me, and when I came back to Mexico I felt that I had improved. I had seen another aspect of the dance, another world, another possibility.

I was invited to Denver again in 1964 to perform in their summer season. This time they paid me more, so I stayed longer in New York and took classes again with American Ballet Theatre and with Joffrey, where I was offered a scholarship. I consulted with Michael Lland who was teaching at Joffrey, and with Bill Griffith who was teaching at American Ballet Theatre. Both told me, 'Don't take Joffrey's scholarship. That's not the company for you — American Ballet Theatre is for you!' Perhaps they saw what I didn't see in myself because they had more experience and better eyes. American Ballet Theatre was on tour and when they returned they held auditions. I took an audition, was accepted, and I signed my contract on December 29, 1964. I stayed with the company for fourteen years, becoming a soloist in 1968 and a principal dancer in 1973.

In 1966, my second year with the company, we went to Russia and some of us brought back several icons. They were not in very good

138

shape and so I started working on mine. When my friends saw the results, they asked if I could do theirs. It all started on an informal basis, and I never thought of it as a profession. To me, these were objects of beauty which I felt deserved to be seen as the artist originally intended.

I enjoyed performing with the company, but as time went on I found myself observing how the profession and the company were changing. A sense of dissatisfaction began to take hold. I observed that dance was becoming more like a business. More and more ballet companies were springing up like mushrooms. The dancers all wanted an opportunity to dance, but without a good technical background and a general awareness of the arts that surrounded them their careers lasted a very short time. Anyone can learn some gimmicks and make a living out of that, but that's not necessarily a career. I also saw that we were becoming more and more like machines, quick effects to fill a program or an evening. You would come out of the theatre and not remember what you just saw because there was nothing for your intellect to grasp. Audiences, as much as they want to be pleased visually, want to be moved and challenged intellectually. Instead, neither the audiences nor the performers were using their intellect. As a result, dancers were growing used to learning and forgetting quickly, and so were the audiences!

Around this time (I think it was in 1979), a friend of mine who owns an art gallery asked me to try and restore a corner of a very beautiful and valuable portrait. I did it as a favor and he was extremely pleased. He began to give me more work and to refer people to me. Finally I decided to leave American Ballet Theatre, and luckily by that time I was already capable of making a living by doing restoration work. I say luckily because as a child in art class in Mexico we were never given tubes of paint, so I had learned how to mix colors and had become familiar with the results of color combinations. I did quite a bit of research on my own and sometimes just figured it out. It's rewarding work but very painstaking, and it requires a great deal of patience.

I have also worked in the area of costume design. I have designed costumes for American Ballet Theatre, the San Francisco Ballet, the Royal Winnipeg Ballet, the Ballet of Caracas, the Delta Festival Ballet of New Orleans, and the North Carolina School of the Arts. It's an area that I work in quite naturally, and I enjoy it very much.

Sometimes when I'm working, I hear some piece of music that I danced to playing on the radio, and I can feel the movements that I used to perform. I miss dancing because it's a joy. To be on the stage is almost like a sacrificial rite, something very, very unique. Also, the profession is so very different in its lifestyle. Being in a ballet company has been likened to being in a family. It's a communal life, and now I am working in one of the most solitary of professions.

Something draws me back to the ballet, however, and I wouldn't be surprised if I eventually returned to a ballet company as a teacher or a coach. If it happens, I will be most willing to give everything of my experience and my knowledge to others, to younger generations. I love to teach and I love children. They are like little jewels. A child is also like a sponge, and is willing to absorb any knowledge that he can get. It's up to the teachers to help fill up this sponge, because if the teachers don't do it the student grows handicapped intellectually. Teachers have to know that a child is willing and sometimes doesn't have the courage to ask. It's up to the teachers to expose students to all the arts, because all the knowledge we acquire can contribute to our performing. It's also important for the students to be aware that not all of them will become dancers. He or she may become an actor, painter, architect, dance teacher, or choreographer, and, when it is realized that one may not be the dancer one has set out to be, the disappointment and frustration will be less.

Recently, I was invited to teach in Japan at the Kyoto Ballet Academy. I was so pleased by the idea that I could again be connected with the ballet world that I became quite indifferent to the pieces of art that were waiting for my attention. I rolled them up, put them in a file, and I left for Japan. I have always liked Japan, its culture and its people. It's a totally different world. I had some difficulty at first because all the levels (beginners, intermediate, and advanced) were put together. Later I learned more about the Japanese educational system, and that they do this so the beginner can copy from the advanced or professional. It's like that in the universities, in every-thing, because they think that in that way the beginner doesn't have the stigma of being different. At the same time, the advanced students coach the beginners. It's a wonderful way of working.

On my last day, at the end of my first class, the students bowed to the pianist, applauded, and left. The second group came in, finished the class, 'respects, congratulations, thank you very much, we'll miss you,' and left the room. While I was teaching the third group, I saw at the end of that class that the two previous groups were looking through the glass doors, and I thought that maybe they planned to come altogether and applaud. They all came in very quietly and made a circle around me, and then one of them gave me an enormous bouquet of flowers. The next day they all came to the train station because I was leaving to visit another city. I was very moved by all this and I found it very hard to leave.

It's difficult now because I find that art restoration has become more like a way to make a living, giving me very little for my spirit. I'm a creative person, like every performer, and I don't want to see myself confined in a room, ending my years of activity in front of a piece of art. I want to continue producing something with my intellect or with my hands. If my feet can't move I'll use my hands and my mouth to communicate.

Dancers believe in that particular magic moment of being on the stage, of moving people's emotions, and we can't deprive ourselves of that because we like to give. I frankly don't know if I see teaching and coaching as my future, but I would love to try it. I need to keep growing. The world of performing is a continuous growing process. Every single night, every performance we give, is an opportunity to grow. Even if we do the same ballet fifty times, we cannot do it the same way. That process has to translate into life."

# WENDY REISER

*"I still feel sad when I think about dance, but the point is to just go on with your life, and that loss becomes a part of life like anything else. I feel very fortunate now that I've had all those experiences, for I have some very good memories of the time when I was dancing."*

*Photograph by Andrew Oxenham*

144

*Photograph by Marilyn Westlake*

*Wendy started taking ballet classes in Stratford, Ontario, when she was three, and at ten won a scholarship to the National Ballet School in Toronto. At fourteen, Wendy accompanied Betty Oliphant, the Artistic Director and Principal of the school, who was guest teaching at the Royal Swedish Opera Ballet. She had been chosen to demonstrate the nature of the training at Canada's National Ballet School. Two years later, Wendy joined the National Ballet of Canada and soon became a soloist, dancing with the company for seven and a half years.*

*After experiencing many difficulties imposed by frequent injuries, Wendy stopped dancing and began to study with the intention of becoming a doctor. She upgraded her pre-university studies and enrolled at Brock University, St. Catharines. By June 1984, six years after leaving the National Ballet, she had achieved her goal. Wendy now has a family practice in a small town near Toronto and is a member of the Board of Directors of the Dancer Transition Centre. She is married to Stuart Laughton and they have two children, Patrick and Jane.*

"I started dancing in Stratford, Ontario, when I was three years old. My family then moved to Hamilton, Ontario, and I applied for the first scholarship to the National Ballet School ever offered by the Hamilton Branch of the National Ballet Guild. I was only ten at the time, and I think my parents had very mixed feelings about my leaving home. But I won the scholarship and went to the school the following fall, starting in Grade 7. It was a strange time for my family because my younger sister had just been born and there was a new baby in the house. Since I had previously been the baby and was now actually leaving home, it was difficult for all of us to adjust. I started at the ballet school, but it was hard for me because I had such strong ties with my parents that I constantly wanted to be home with them. At the same time I had this burning drive to be a ballet dancer.

In 1967, Betty Oliphant, the Artistic Director and Principal of the school, was invited by Erik Bruhn to teach at the Royal Swedish Opera Ballet. He wanted to model the school in Sweden after the National Ballet School. Miss Oliphant felt that she needed to take a student along with her so that she could demonstrate that the things she was telling people there were feasible. I went along as an example of the training that was going on in Canada, which in retrospect was quite an honor. I had a wonderful time. The first day I was there I did ballet class with Erik Bruhn watching and Margot Fonteyn and Rudolph Nureyev taking the class. I was only fourteen, but I knew people were looking at this little girl from Canada. I couldn't concentrate — I was too excited. After my experience in Sweden, I found it difficult to come back to Toronto because my teachers singled me out with a lot of attention and my classmates were often jealous. As a result I became more unhappy, particularly since I was still not living at home at the time and I missed having the support of my family. I was at the ballet school for seven years, and I don't think I really adjusted until I was almost sixteen. But by then my parents had moved to Toronto, I had moved back home, and I had come to some sort of terms with my life as a dancer.

Although I had found life hard at the ballet school, I joined the National Ballet of Canada at seventeen, and I discovered that life in the company was equally difficult. When you're a 'star' of the school and then go into the company, you find yourself in the corps de ballet. In ballet class at the school everybody got lots of corrections and you came to expect that. You're not used to the independence of professional company life and, even though you learn to work on your own, it's at a very different level to that of the student. Dancers have to make that transition to working independently within the company; if not, you just don't survive. It takes time and a great deal of adjustment to discover how to work at that level.

I was quickly promoted to first soloist and danced with the company for seven and a half years. However, my career was hampered by a lot of injuries, including a couple of serious fractures. Once you start on that roller coaster of hurting yourself it becomes very frustrating. There were many times when I didn't feel all that happy, but this was when everybody was feeling unhappy. We were performing a lot. I was in the company in the early seventies when we were doing a lot of 'Sleeping Beauties.' We performed every night for months, had two shows on Saturdays and Sundays and it was extremely tiring. In preparing for these performances we worked a lot with Rudolph Nureyev. He's a giant, a very great artist. He was also a lot of fun and he got along very well with the company.

I think the final thing for me was that I somehow realized that my mental health was starting to fail. I was getting extremely depressed far too often, coming home almost every night in tears. At that time, however, I had a good sounding board. I was engaged to be married and my fiancé was terrific at listening to me and in trying to present the situation as it really was. I remember when we sat down together and he said, 'Well, what would happen if you quit?' I couldn't really think of anything bad that would happen. It wasn't as if I was suddenly going to drop dead or the whole world was going to collapse. We decided that although I would quit, I wouldn't do it by burning my bridges. I talked to Alexander Grant, our Artistic Director at the time, and said that I was really unhappy and would like to stop dancing. I left the company with the feeling that I could go back if I found that I wanted to.

I'm very fortunate to have a husband like Stuart Laughton. He's a classical trumpet player and was a member of the orchestra on one occasion on a tour. That's where we met. I think we had been going out for a year and a half before I stopped dancing. He's a very level-headed man and a gifted performer. He knows the kind of commitment it takes to be an artist and at the same time has good insight into what living is all about. I think he has established a very good balance between his art and his private life.

When I first left the company I was elated. I think it was the first time in my life that I had stood up for myself and said what amounted to 'I don't want to do what you're telling me to do anymore — I'm not happy.' It was also the first time I actually acknowledged that I was unhappy, and when I took action there was a feeling of control. For the first few weeks I was very busy trying to see what sort of options were available to me. I went to Manpower (the Canadian Government Ministry of Employment and Immigration) and they said, 'What do you do?' I said, 'I'm a dancer.' 'Well, we don't have any jobs for dancers.' I had some ideas about how I would like to re-train, what sort of things I thought might interest me, although even that was difficult because I had never considered what I would do if I weren't a dancer.

I felt that I wouldn't be happy if I didn't find another career. Staying at home and being a mother and a wife is not enough for me. Even now when I stay home for a few days I can't wait to get back to my work. The obvious thing to do was to go to the National Ballet School and learn to be a teacher. However, I was feeling so bad about ballet at that time that I really didn't want to do that. I didn't see teaching as my future and I never even inquired about it. I was very close to Betty Oliphant, and when I think about it now teaching would have been a natural thing to do, but I just didn't want to do it!

I had been injured a lot during my dancing career and I'd had a lot of contact with members of the health profession: doctors, physiotherapists, and chiropractors. It was an area that I knew something about. When I thought a little more about it, I knew it would be incredibly difficult for me to become a doctor. Here I was, a twenty-four year old, with no education beyond Grade 12 and no sciences since Grade 10. It seemed as though I had the cards stacked against me, but I think the challenge of it was part of the appeal. I knew that if I was going to do that, I'd have to totally commit myself. I think now that the process was therapeutic for me. It helped me to work through my loss.

I was very calculating about how I proceeded. I knew that to get into medical school I had to have very high marks, and that before going to medical school I had to complete certain university courses. The first thing I did was a pre-university course in which I achieved 95%. By passing that I got into university as a mature student. Then I did a Grade 13 chemistry course at night school during the summer because I knew that to go to medical school I had to do science subjects. I figured that to get high marks at university I had to have some science background. When I went to university I went to a small one — Brock University in St. Catharines. I knew that if I went there and discovered that I had problems, I would get attention. There would be time for a professor to sit down and explain things to me and I didn't think I would get lost in the masses. I also knew that I would have to do very well and work extremely hard.

I completed two years at Brock University, a minimum requirement, and then entered the University of Toronto Faculty of Medicine. I graduated from medical school in June 1984, having had my first child two years before. Now I have a family practice in the Niagara Peninsula where I'm close to an academic center with a lot of resources. I love working with people and I love the continuity of family medicine. The only other part of my life I have to make time for now is my family — my husband, Stuart, and my children, Patrick and Jane.

I still don't have a complete understanding of my own situation and the nature of my transition. However, I do continue to think about the ballet a great deal. I was listening recently to a program on grieving and death, and I noticed that my relationship with the ballet now feels like I have experienced a death. I feel like I've lost a very close sister. While it sometimes seems strange to me that I got involved so quickly in another profession, I do feel that my medical career has helped me get over my loss. I realize now that life goes on and one makes the most of it.

I think my having a family has actually made things easier because, with other lives involved, I simply had to get myself back on track. If you leave dance because you're clear that you want to do something else, it's probably easier. Sometimes, you need new input to help you sort things out. I think that if you box yourself in and don't do anything, then you tend to worry and dwell too much on your situation. It really depends on why a dancer has left dancing. I left because I was unhappy and frustrated and I felt that I had a lot of talent that wasn't being used. It was a bad time for me and it was a very bad time for the National Ballet of Canada.

Before I stopped dancing I had thought about going to another company and going to Europe, but I fell in love! I was just so fed up and angry with the ballet that I didn't want to have anything more to do with it. My attention was focused on my personal life, and I think that's the reason I didn't pick up and go somewhere else right away. In any event, I think it probably is difficult to do that because one has such a protected life in the company. It's difficult because it's all you know, your whole life. You're not aware of the rest of the world going on around you, and then suddenly you're out into that world and it's as if you've landed on Mars.

I don't think such a transition is any easier today. Dancers still apply the same kind of dedication, and more than anything else I think it's the dancer's intense emotional involvement that creates the problems. For example, I was out for five or six months at one stretch with an injury, and during that time I saw nobody I knew. Occasionally someone would call and make sure I was okay, but I didn't want to go out because I was feeling bad about being injured and no one seemed to really care that I had slipped out of the mainstream. It was a shock! The 'family' feeling is there when you're working, and when you're seeing people every day you feel part of that community. It's difficult when you're suddenly removed from that, either through injury or because you've decided to quit dancing. The more established companies now make it possible to have a more balanced lifestyle, and their dancers may be a bit broader in the way they view life. Of course, the times are different too. It's now possible to be a dancer and see it as a job. Although it's your career and you take pride in that, it's now acceptable to have a family and to have another life.

The 'message' of my story is that I just went on with my life and tried to let my feelings sort themselves out as I went along. After eight years now they're still in some turmoil. I still experience feelings of sadness, loss, and grief. When my mother died five years ago, I felt in many ways as I did when I stopped dancing. The initial period of loss was just so awful, but now, when I think about my mother, I have good memories and I can enjoy thinking about her. I still feel sad when I think about dance, but the point is to just go on with your life, and that loss becomes a part of life like anything else. I feel very fortunate now that I've had all those experiences, for I have some very good memories of the time when I was dancing. I would never not have been a dancer; it was terrific. It's made me the person I am and I'm very happy and proud of that. I know that I have achieved what I have because of all my early training and discipline, and I know that I'm becoming the kind of committed doctor that I am because of my ballet experience."

# NANCY REYNOLDS

*"I think that a lot of people spend their lives preparing to prepare to do something, but if you jump in and try to swim, you often get farther because there's no alternative but to swim."*

*Photograph by Martha Swope*

*Photograph by Erik Schweikhardt*

## EXCHANGES: LIFE AFTER DANCE

*Nancy Reynolds began her dance studies in New York at the King-Coit Children's Theatre School, and continued at the School of American Ballet and with Vera Nemtchinova, Maria Swoboda, and Carmelita Maracci. She joined the New York City Ballet in 1956 and danced there for five years. After leaving in 1961, she studied for a semester at the Sorbonne in Paris and then returned to the U.S. to attend Columbia University, graduating Phi Beta Kappa in 1965 with a degree in art history.*

*From 1965 to 1971 Nancy worked for Praeger Publishers as an associate editor of the Art Book Division, editor of the Dance Book Program, and managing editor of Art Reference. A collaboration with Lincoln Kirstein, as his editor for* Movement and Metaphor: Four Centuries of Ballet *(New York:Praeger, 1970) awakened her interest in dance writing, and particularly in dance history. Since leaving Praeger, Nancy has formed her own company for the production of a slide history of dance and has worked as a freelance writer, researcher, and editor for art and dance books and journals. Her publications include* Repertory in Review: Forty Years of the New York City Ballet *(New York: Dial, 1977),* The Dance Catalog: A Complete Guide to Today's World of Dance *(New York: Harmony, 1979), and* In Performance: A Companion to the Classics of the Dance *(New York: Harmony, 1980). Nancy was also Research Director for the landmark publication* Choreography by George Balanchine: A Catalogue of Works *(Harvey Simmonds, Ed., New York: Eakins Press Foundation, 1983), the first catalogue raisonné to be devoted to a choreographer. In the same year she again worked with Lincoln Kirstein, providing an introduction to and commentaries on a collection of his dance writings,* Ballet: Bias and Belief *(New York: Dance Horizons, 1983). She was then made Research Director for public television's two-hour documentary* Balanchine. *Nancy has lectured at Brooklyn College, the University of Chicago, and Temple University. She has served on many dance-related committees and boards, including the board of the Dance Notation Bureau and the planning committee for the "International Encyclopedia of Dance" (New York: Scribner's, forthcoming). In 1974 she received a Ford Foundation Travel and Study Grant. In 1977 she was awarded the De La Torre Bueno Prize for the best book-length manuscript,* Repertory in Review. *She is married to Brian Rushton and has one son, Ehren.*

"What prompted me to start ballet lessons at age eleven was that while I was in the King-Coit school, Tanaquil LeClercq came to teach. She was about twenty-one, and terribly glamorous, quite unlike the usual non-English-speaking, aged Russians. (I later came to *adore* this breed, but for a first lesson, little could rival the presence of

156

a performing ballerina.) The class was only forty minutes weekly, but because of her I became completely committed to becoming a professional dancer. It turned out that I had extraordinarily good feet and I seemed to show an exceptional affinity for ballet. Almost immediately, I was fired with total enthusiasm and dedication. Through Tanny, I heard of the School of American Ballet (Balanchine's school). I wanted nothing but the best and nothing but the most stringent requirements. No one in my family knew anything about ballet, and there was certainly no guarantee that I would be successful; moreover, I went to a very proper girls' school, and it was not considered very genteel there to be too dedicated to anything. ('Well-roundedness' was the ideal of the day.) Initially, my mother was against such single-minded training, but I finally talked her into it.

By the time I was sixteen, however, problems emerged which eventually caused me to give up dancing. Things began to go badly for no reason that one could name. I had insomnia, and my grades started to slip. It was, I'm sure, partly just becoming an adult, but also the need to make some extremely important life decisions at a very young age. But, in fact, I wasn't really young enough. I was too old and knew too much to forge blindly ahead, and yet I knew that this was just what was required for the profession. At fifteen everything had been fine. At sixteen, everything was wrong. Dancing held me in a very tight grip. Many dancers have solved this — that is, they have managed to put their dancing into some kind of perspective that allowed them to breathe rather than to suffocate — but I was never able to. Everything was deadly serious, even desperate. But I was still totally committed to being a dancer. However, along with the psychological distress such a regimented existence was causing me, I was beginning to find out that my physical 'equipment' was not as terrific as I had thought. It was good for some things, but not for others. I was much too flexible and I was always weak. (Many years later, Balanchine sent me to Martha Graham to see if she could do anything about strengthening my back.) I couldn't do pirouettes and I couldn't balance. My exceedingly high insteps were a great handicap in executing quick footwork, although they looked gorgeous in battement tendu. It was the same with hyperextended knees: I looked great standing around, but I began to realize — very late, I think — how much more was involved in really *dancing*. And I wasn't good at it.

However, I was just as devoted as ever; my increasing awareness of my technical deficiencies did not in any way reduce my zeal or my desire to master it all. For all my unhappiness, my drive never wavered. Although nobody in my family approved of what I was doing — another source of anguish — I was determined to become a dancer even if I had to be in the corps de ballet my entire life!

So I trained and trained and eventually I got into the New York City Ballet. But the terrible part was that with ballet every day is like every other day, mostly physical drudgery and self-flagellation. So getting into the company was not like taking a quantum leap into a new world. It was really just a small step from what I had already been doing. Joining the New York City Ballet did not produce the kind of elation that you might imagine. It was just one tiny increment in a kind of progression that I'd worked very hard on for many, many years. The discovery that this was so was, of course, devastating.

I danced with the New York City Ballet for five years, from 1956 to 1961 — always questioning why I was doing it — and when I decided to leave, it was mainly because I didn't want to dance anymore. Also, after working with Balanchine, I felt it wasn't possible for me to dance anywhere else. (There were not nearly so many other companies to choose from then as there are now, although I did have offers from Bob Joffrey and Todd Bolender.) It was partly, also, that I found the life of a dancer a tormented exercise. I was tired and depressed all the time. I felt I was putting everything into it and getting very little back. I didn't feel particularly comfortable on stage, and I didn't think I was attaining the ideal I felt so strongly about. I was constantly falling short, and boundaries of all kinds were closing in. On a more prosaic level, I didn't like not knowing my schedule. While I never had to live out of a suitcase, I couldn't make any day-to-day plans, and I felt I was on call like a puppet. Although I was fascinated by what Balanchine was doing, I viewed my own dancing as a series of muscular endeavors. To make matters worse, I was never in control of my technique and felt that without the mirror I couldn't really sense what I was doing. I didn't know what I looked like, and I didn't know what kind of an impression I was making. I didn't have a feel for theatre, and I just never found the glorious release in dancing that so many do.

All of this was a big shock after so many years of effort. I felt that if dancing were reduced to a matter of staying in line with a lot of other girls, then I wasn't interested. I had been brought up to work, hone, and polish my purely technical equipment to the best of my ability with no thought about anything else. I don't think I realized how much more there was to dancing until many years after I had stopped.

I think I was too aware of my lacks, unable to roll with the punches to see what might happen, and very intense about knowing exactly what I was doing, so I was inflexible.

Leaving the company was certainly not a hastily made decision or an arbitrary one. I wanted very much to go to college, partly because my family pushed and pushed, and partly because I felt there was something else out there, although I didn't know what. So within six weeks of my final performance I was enrolled in Columbia's summer school, and I was so excited about what I was doing that dancing didn't seem relevant. I was very lucky not to go through a long period of trying to discover myself. In fact, much of that painful self-discovery was done while I was dancing, because I had been so ill-suited there. Of course, I took chances. I think that a lot of people spend their lives preparing to prepare to do something, but if you jump in and try to swim, you often get farther because there's no alternative *but* to swim. There's something Balanchine said which is perfect (especially if you're young, as I was — later, you have less to throw away): 'What does it matter if you die tomorrow? At least do one step full out today.' In one way, college for me was very like dancing — something I could embrace tightly.

After graduating with an art major, I continued to be idealistic and wanted to spend my life in an ivory tower, 'intellectualizing.' (I despised the physical at that point.) But I had a lot of pressure from my mother and others to get a job. So, instead of going to graduate school, I went to typing school! Another dancer's husband was starting a little publishing company after hours, and for about six months I typed labels for him and sorted invoices, while listening to him talk about what he wanted to accomplish in publishing. It was a whole new world and definitely something you couldn't learn in school. The tremendous benefit of it was that, when I finally passed my typing test and had to decide what to do next, I was already sold on publishing. So in two ways I was lucky: because of the stimulation of college, abandoning dance did not leave a wrenching void; and, almost by accident, without years of searching, I fell into another profession — publishing — one which, as I was to discover, had some of the same psychological components as dancing (although not in so extreme a form), notably, service to a higher cause than oneself — in this case, literature.

I was offered two entry-level publishing jobs at eighty dollars a week. Even in 1965, that wasn't too good! I chose Praeger, which had an art-book department. I didn't mind the typing, filing, or any of that because it was all new and different, and I was learning something. I also found I was thrilled to be in the commercial world. I'd never thought about commerce, but I soon discovered that it's a major moving force in the existence of all of us.

I then met the man who was to become my husband. He had a background in merchandising as well as in production and editing. (I was in the editorial side of things.) From him I learned that the sales and promotion people could be just as creative in their fields as were the editorial people who brought in the book ideas — another stimulating discovery. For me all this seemed to have a relevance to 'real life' that dancing never had. It was even possible to be concerned with something other than oneself.

While working for Praeger, I edited Lincoln Kirstein's book, *Movement and Metaphor*. At first, he didn't remember me from the company, but after three years of working with him, he did remember. When I was dancing and studying, I had almost never read any dance books. In fact, I consciously avoided them because dancing already possessed me to the point of claustrophobia. In college, writing for me had to do with great intellectual concepts, not with sweaty, mindless dancing. Then in walked Mr. Kirstein with his astounding manuscript, which combined his philosophy of dance and performance, the history of four hundred years of ballet, his personal critical sense, incredible illustrations, and the wealth of his own fantastic and mercurial self. Although I am not a child of the 'sixties,' for once I can use one of those 'hip' expressions because it is here completely apt: the experience truly 'blew my mind.' It was as though my head had been screwed on in a different way.

Working with Lincoln showed me that one could write meaningfully about dance. By the time I had finished three years' work with him, I could see that a brain could be used to say something and to do something in the service of dance. It was an inspiration. I got to know him a little as well. He seems a gruff and forbidding man, but underneath it all is a warm, sweet streak. While he's not given to small talk, he was marvellously co-operative and appreciative of everything I did. And he's a man of monumental action as well as thought — the rarest of combinations.

After *Movement and Metaphor*, I left Praeger. It was a bad period for the publishing industry, and I had begun to chafe at the office hours. But now I had acquired a skill that I could sell by the hour, and I started doing freelance editing, mostly of art books. When Lincoln heard I was available, he asked if I would like to edit one of the New York City Ballet's souvenir booklets. I said yes. The theme was the Balanchine-Stravinsky collaboration, which I prepared under his guidance. About this time, he was approached about doing a book on the repertory of the New York City Ballet; he suggested that I could be the author. So, out of the clear blue sky I had a contract to write a book! I had never visualized myself a writer; I was more interested in working with someone else's good writing than with writing myself. I was scared to death, but after thinking it over for some time, I came to the conclusion that no one was going to offer me such an opportunity again. I had also discovered that the life of a freelance editor was rather lonely: I was spending a great deal of time in the library checking facts, not talking above a whisper, and I wasn't too happy with that. So I decided I'd take a chance and do the book. Five years and countless hours of soul-searching later, it was published.

Two things happened in the course of doing the book: one was that I learned an enormous amount about the history of the New York City Ballet, most of which I had been quite unaware of as a performer, and the other was what I found in interviewing the dancers. With dancers I could begin in the middle. There was so much that did not need saying; we were already on a common wavelength. Most of the dancers I had known — and had virtually lived with during tours — had never told me much about their feelings about dancing. It had all been about feet and bunions, but how people felt about their lives, and particularly about their art, had never been discussed. I felt I made a far more intimate acquaintance with some of these people as a non-performer than I had when sharing the stage with them. This provided me with a kind of emotional substance that had always seemed to be missing from the dancer's life — at least, the dancer's life as I had experienced it.

By the time the book came out, I had begun to be involved in other aspects of the dance world. I was introduced to the education scene and I realized for the first time that there was dance in other places besides New York! (How silly that sounds, but as a dancer, I truly lived in a tunnel.) I met Selma Jeanne Cohen, the 'doyenne' of dance historians. (Lincoln must be considered 'hors concours'.) She is the first person I know of who embraced dance history as a profession, not a sideline. In one of her classes someone mentioned the need for teaching materials. I knew from my art-history lectures what it meant to use slides rather than just talk. In dance there were no illustrated materials; teachers held up books and pointed to black and white photographs to show 'dancing.' So I formed a tiny company, a business partnership, and produced a slide history of twentieth-century dance. I think that was quite a contribution. (It also turned out to be more financially rewarding than writing books!)

When he saw *Repertory in Review*, Balanchine was very anxious to send a copy to a boyhood friend in Russia, the noted dance critic Yuri Slonimsky. This was the first clue that he had an interest in anything written about him — with Balanchine, dancing had always been the common language, and if you didn't speak it, you were outside his world. But as he got older, he realized that there were people in his life who had been unable to see his dances, who had missed out on his entire development, and that there was no way he could show them that development except through a book. Perhaps the time had come to approach him about a *catalogue raisonné* of his astonishingly varied and prolific output, some 425 known works in all. (At an earlier date, he would merely have sniffed at the idea.)

The time was right. I was engaged by the Eakins Press Foundation to direct a team of researchers all over the world, whose job was to collect as much documentation as possible about every dance, of every type, Balanchine had created: opera divertissements, television, impromptu numbers in private homes, student dances performed on outdoor platforms — as well as some of the most supreme achievements in the dance of this century. The idea was to be thorough and comprehensive because, whether our results turned out to be good or bad, since we were doing it no one else would attempt to gather this information again for years — until long after Balanchine and many of his most important interpreters were gone.

Balanchine was enthusiastic and accessible, and he had an incredible memory. He seemed quite amused at some of the things we uncovered from some sixty years ago. (The idea was to 'excavate' as thoroughly as possible from whatever sources we could find, then take the results to Mr. B. for confirmation or cross-checking or as a memory jog.) In addition to his inspiring participation (and that of others), the project was a dream because it had wonderful funding and backing. So, in addition to the importance of the subject, we had a substantial budget. It was a project that motivated people. There was never any need to demonstrate its significance or explain why it was essential to do it now. So everyone was eager to contribute.

Balanchine's active assistance was a kind of cornerstone; we were able to contact people who had worked with him in the 20s, 30s, 40s, 50s, 60s, 70s, and 80s (along with Tamara Geva, Alexandra Danilova, and Pyotr Gusev, who had known him as a teenager!) — people from virtually every stage of his career. Because of lavish funding, we had access to scholars, librarians, and archives in all parts of the world. Where Balanchine was concerned, no effort seemed too great, no lead too small to be followed up. He saw a proof copy of the book in the hospital before he died. He called it 'the Bible.'

The chronology was published in 1983. As Jerome Robbins said, 'To be aware of the total span of Balanchine's work is an astonishing and awesome experience.' As you can imagine, working on a book like that was incredibly meaningful for me. My other obvious feeling is, thank God we've got it. Starting just one year later would have made it too late to talk to him. When we began, Balanchine was not ill and no one could have known the exact amount of time we would have, but everybody felt the urgency of the undertaking.

Since the chronology, I've been involved in several things. It's important for me to have some variety and, as writing can be very solitary, my work has often involved other people in some way; while I still want to do research and writing, I'm also interested in jobs that require administration and management of other people's abilities. One of the exciting things about dance scholarship, history, and research is that it's a new field and people are constantly doing things you've never thought of before. It's extremely stimulating to talk with the people who are doing these things. It also provides a new approach to scholarship — one in which the living participants, tapes, videos, notation, and all kinds of visual material (museum collections of costumes, for example) are just as important as the printed sources venerated in other academic fields. Dance history is not encrusted with or straightjacketed by tradition. This is wonderful for the adventurous, but can also yield some very uneven work. We are still setting the standards.

My current project is a narrative history of dance in the twentieth century — by far my biggest undertaking from a writing point of view. I guess it will either crown my career with glory or bury me well in advance of my old age! For all the scope it provides for intellectual investigation, writing, like dancing, is a very insecure profession. But at least you don't have to look good while you are grappling with the computer, waiting for those blessed words to come. No one but a dancer would know just how much of a relief that is."

163

# JAMES RONALDSON

*"When dancing became just a job for me, I stopped. As a dancer, I had a lot of faith in myself and a lot of will and drive. When I later got to a point where I questioned whether I wanted to continue in wardrobe, Celia Franca said, 'You ought to make up your mind; either settle down and take your job seriously, or quit!' I realized she was right and started working with commitment."*

165

*Photograph by Ken Bell*

*Photograph by Marilyn Westlake*

## EXCHANGES: LIFE AFTER DANCE

*Montreal-born, James made a late start for a dancer, beginning his training when he was seventeen. Before this he had studied fashion design, and was able to use his skills to support himself throughout his dance training. In Montreal, he performed at ballet festivals, participated in regional competitions, and joined the ballet of the Metropolitan Opera Company when they performed there. He then spent a year studying in London, England, during which time he was hired for the movie* Charlie's Aunt.

*On returning to Canada, James danced at the Canadian National Exhibition and then auditioned for the National Ballet of Canada. He was accepted into the company and danced with them for five years. During that time he also danced in television productions. Discovering that he no longer wanted to perform, James offered to run the wardrobe at the National Ballet and went on to manage and develop this department through a long period of growth in the company. He was able to bring a rare sense of movement possibility to his work and has contributed enormously to the development of one of the best wardrobe departments in ballet. James recently retired due to ill health.*

"I'm from Montreal, and I can remember seeing the Ballet Russe de Monte Carlo and Ballet Theatre there when I was about sixteen. At that time I preferred the Ballet Russe. I found them more theatrical. They were really exciting performers. I thought Ballet Theatre looked a bit stuffy in comparison. The result, though, was that I decided that I wanted to dance professionally. My family felt that, if I wanted to do that, then I had to pay for it myself. For some reason, I kept putting it off. I just couldn't seem to get myself to a class. One day a friend of mine, Katharine Burnett, just simply made me go. She dragged me off to class, and after that I enjoyed classes very much and continued to train.

I was seventeen when I started to take classes, and with such a late start I discovered that it hurt a lot. But I worked hard, did summer schools, and after a while I didn't need to pay for lessons because I was doing the books, collecting the money from the students and things like that. I performed at amateur ballet festivals and took part in regional competitions. That was the extent of the performing opportunities, since this was all before 1952. I was training in a country which at that time didn't have any professional performing opportunities. My intention was to go to Broadway and work in musicals.

We did have ballet festivals though. The third ballet festival in Canada was held in Montreal, and schools came from all over the country to participate. The schools had developed little ballet companies, and that was the dance climate in Canada which supported the founding of the National Ballet in 1951. Of course, we weren't paid for these performances. I also danced with the Metropolitan Opera Company when they were playing in Montreal. Local dancers were hired to supplement the cast, and I got through those performances on pure nerve. I barely remembered what I'd done because I was so nervous. After that, I decided to go to England. I just wanted to get away from everything in Montreal.

I'd studied the R.A.D. method in Montreal and I knew that I could continue my training in England. I studied there with Anna Northcote. I loved her and learned more from her than anyone else. She said, 'If you will take my beginners' class, which you will pay for, all other daily classes will be free.' So I took three or four classes a day. I spent the whole day in class! About that time I did the movie *Charlie's Aunt* with Ray Bolger. The movie was made in London and I'd been hired to do the pre-rehearsals, where Ray was going to try the steps out. I'd been hired by the movie people strictly for my face. They didn't know whether I could dance a step! After a while I really didn't want to stay in London any longer. I'd had enough of the rotten weather, plaster falling off the ceiling in the school, and the cold. I decided that I'd come home.

Back in Canada, the Canadian National Exhibition was coming up and I went to Toronto to audition for the choreographer, Alan Lund. I was hired. During that time, I met Kay Ambrose, an extraordinary woman who was a designer and did publicity. You name it, she did it! While I was in rehearsal, the tutus they were making were all falling down and Kay asked me to help. I guess by then she knew that I could sew. I'd taken a design course before I went into ballet. At that time I had wanted to be a designer of fashion clothes, and the skills I learned enabled me to pay for my ballet lessons and living expenses. The National Ballet had been formed during the year I was in England, and Kay convinced me that I should stay in Toronto and audition for the company. I took an audition, was accepted, and one of the first roles I did was The Man She Must Marry in *Lilac Garden*. I enjoyed doing *Lilac Garden* and, after a period of adjustment, liked working with Antony Tudor very much. I danced with the company for five years, but after a while I started to count how many *Lilac Gardens*, *Swan Lakes*, and *Coppelias* I had to do, and I knew I didn't want to do them anymore. I found performing far too nerve-wracking. Eventually, I completely

169

stopped enjoying performing.

It was, however, an interesting era at the National Ballet. We definitely thought we were building something of value. Had it not been for Celia Franca I don't think we would have stuck it out — we were starving and we made nothing. We all believed in Celia Franca and in the National Ballet. We also had a fabulous Board of Directors in those days. They were personally involved with us and were there all the time. They came to rehearsals and very often paid us themselves when the company couldn't afford to. It was a wonderful group. We competed, naturally, but we were all friends and we lived in a very small community. We came from all parts of Canada; we had no money and no friends outside the company. I hated the lack of money and the discomfort of it all, and I was the first one to go out and get a television job in the summer. Brian Macdonald was the choreographer, and we did three or four live numbers a week. This work paid about twenty times what I was making at the National. Sometimes I would also do a weekly program called *L'Heure du Concert*, so I was making very good money at that time.

I danced with the National Ballet for about five years, and during that time I quit once. That was the year I was doing *L'Heure du Concert* in Montreal, and I was going to get a contract from CBC to continue with that program. The money was so good, the work was regular, and at that time the National Ballet didn't perform much and we only got paid when we worked. There was no union then, and there were no unemployment benefits available. Parents helped many of the dancers survive and many dancers had other jobs. One of the dancers used to dig ditches on lay-offs! So I quit! Then Celia sent me a telegram asking, did I want to reconsider and rejoin the company? I gave it about ten minutes thought and said yes. I didn't want to stay in Montreal and my personal life was a bit chaotic. So I came back to Toronto and the National.

Finally though, I reached a point where I'd had enough, and I asked Celia if she would allow me to run the wardrobe, as no one was doing that. More often than not I couldn't stand the fit of my costumes, and I felt sure that I could do them better. She agreed. I remember I went to her and said that I wanted $55 a week, and she said I'd be earning as much as the principal dancers! This was one time that I didn't back down, and I got the $55. I stayed until I took a year off to go to Europe, and when I returned I really developed the wardrobe. I enjoyed the work very, very much. As the company grew, so did the budgets for the costumes, and we worked harder because we had to produce more. Since the production of *Romeo and Juliet* in 1964, I've never had to worry about budgets or money for the wardrobe. While I did have to do a lot of begging for *Nutcracker*, the people I was begging from were on the Board of Directors, and they led me to other people who would give me fabric and leather and things like that. I haven't had to do that kind of thing in recent years.

The wardrobe at the National Ballet is one of the best in the world of ballet, and I think I have a knack of choosing the kind of people who will be right for the department. Most wardrobe people come untrained in ballet, and costumes for ballet are very different from those for theatre. Oddly enough, by being involved with the movement possibilities of costuming and having been a dancer, I seem to have limited my creativity as a designer. I don't think the two go together. Some of the best results come from designers who don't know anything about the movement aspect and who leave the technicalities and problems for someone else to solve. They say something like, 'This is my silhouette, this is my texture, this is what I want — now find a way to do it.' I think the best designers have a great deal of imagination. If they can make something magical and help you believe in a make-believe world, they've been successful.

I find that dancers today are perhaps not as dedicated as they have been in the past. They have better technique, better education, more money, and live much more comfortably, and yet I don't get the feeling that dancing is as important as it once seemed to be. I notice that they often complain about going on the stage and, unless they're doing something very special, they don't seem to enjoy it particularly. It's a chore, a job. When dancing became just a job for me, I stopped. As a dancer, I had a lot of faith in myself and a lot of will and drive. When I later got to a point where I questioned whether I wanted to continue in wardrobe, Celia Franca said, 'You ought to make up your mind; either settle down and take your job seriously, or quit!' I realized she was right and I started working with commitment.

I've retired now because of ill health. I'm not rich, and it doesn't seem to matter a hell of a lot. I've had all the emotional life I could handle or want, and I look at what I've built and I'm satisfied. I do wish a dancer had been interested in taking over the wardrobe, however, and my only regret is that I never found one who was. While the department is in good hands, I wish it could have been someone who knew like myself what it feels like to move in a costume."

# ELLEN SHIRE

*"One of the reasons I was unhappy in the company was that I had to take orders from somebody else. I now see the importance of that discipline in creating a vision. But I didn't want to be part of someone else's dream. I wanted to create my own."*

*Photograph by Fred Fehl*

*Photograph by Suzannah Wilshire with permission from Ellen Shire*

*Ellen began her ballet studies in New York with Marina Svetlova and later studied at the School of American Ballet. At seventeen, she was an apprentice with the New York City Ballet. In the following year, 1959, she joined the company, dancing with them for five and a half years. .*

*After leaving in 1965, Ellen worked as an illustrator and wrote children's books. She has had six children's books published. While she continues to write and illustrate from time to time, Ellen now devotes most of her time to painting. At present she lives in Greece six months of the year, returning to New York annually with her work.*


"My mother was a member of Martha Graham's original company. She took me to ballet school because she felt that classical training was the basis of all dance movement. She also took me to ballet performances, and I loved Balanchine ballets from a very early age. I thought that he went beyond the classics and, even though I was very young, I realized that his choreography was a combination of modern dance and ballet.

My mother repeatedly warned me against the professional life of the dancer, having been through a dance career herself and thus being aware of its hardships. She just wanted me to have ballet training to be graceful. She discouraged me from going into the professional life because she thought it was too heartbreaking, too rough, and too competitive. But nothing discouraged me.

My father is a violist who played with the Manhattan String Quartet. He wanted to pursue a solo career, but that became difficult because he had a family to support. Years later, while I was with the New York City Ballet, he often played in the orchestra while I was on stage.

When I was nine, I began two years of training with Marina Svetlova. Then when I was eleven, I auditioned for the School of American Ballet where I was accepted and placed in the beginners' class. I remember that I was quite put out at the time, thinking that after two years of study I certainly should be in the intermediate class! The school was highly competitive, but I was with the best and I wanted to get to the top of the best. Sometimes it was very discouraging. I had a lot to combat physically, such as poor turnout and big feet! But mentally I felt that I had to make it. This was absolutely what I wanted!

I was an apprentice, at the age of seventeen, with the New York

City Ballet and put into the final movement of *Symphony in C*. There were six of us chosen and it was one of the most exciting times of my life. I was thrilled and, fortunately, the performance went quite well. It took another year for me to get into the company and that year was very difficult; I was constantly on edge. I didn't know if I was going to make it or not and, if I didn't make it, where was I to go after that? I really didn't want to be with any other company. I felt that to be with any other would be second best, and I believed that I could make it. Balanchine noticed me a lot in class. I think he liked oddballs. I was lucky; I was tall and I was an oddball.

When I joined the company we were all terrified of Balanchine. He was everything that every dancer talks about, and I felt he was a genius. I would have been happy to have been only in his ballets and to have worked only with him. He held your career in his hands. Working with him on a new ballet was like being a piece of clay in a sculptor's hands, and I loved it! He was easy to work for. He told you what he wanted and made you feel you could do it. But if you ever fought him in any way, you were in trouble. He just would not tolerate it. For example, I'm the daughter of a musician. I grew up in a musical atmosphere and, one day in a rehearsal, Balanchine said, 'Dear (when he was angry with you he always called you *dear*), do you count or do you listen to the music?' I very proudly said, 'I listen to the music!' And he said, 'Well, dear, in my company you count!' And that was that! (But during performance I went by the music!) I often felt he was unfair and very tyrannical. Yet, when you worked with him you forgot that because what he was creating was fantastic.

I had grown up in the school from age eleven, and Balanchine was like a great shadow that you were under. You shivered every time he came into the class. When you saw his feet at the top of the stairs, you knew that that whole class was going to be completely different. So for me, it was conflict all the time. I understand the conflict now because I understand myself better. I have to do my own thing, and I don't let anything stand in the way of what I want to do. One of the reasons I was unhappy in the company was that I had to take orders from somebody else. I now see the importance of that discipline in creating a vision. But I didn't want to be part of someone else's dream. I wanted to create my own.

My mother regretted it when she left Martha Graham and a brief ensuing solo career to raise a family, but I did not regret leaving Balanchine. She felt she had left too soon because she had a great, a very, very great belief in modern dance, in what she was doing and in Graham's genius. (My mother actually went on to become a fine painter, having studied under Will Barnett and Hans Hofmann, among others.) I believed in Balanchine's genius, but I think that I had many more conflicts in the company. The Graham company was brand new. They were the pioneers and they knew they were all shaping something together. Balanchine's company had much more of the atmosphere of a big institution. There were people who absolutely hated it and people who absolutely loved it, as is the case today. The choreography is of a very specialized kind. It has a lot of modern in it, so it attracts a type of person who is already interested in another kind of movement.

I stayed with the company for five and a half years. I found that the studio years, the years of working towards something, are sometimes more fulfilling than when you achieve your dream. After about three years in the company I began to ask myself, 'Is this really what I want?' From that point, when I started to question my reasons for being a dancer, my focus changed and what was once a given became an effort. I used to sit in the park and think about it. I realized that I was enjoying layoffs, and coming back after a layoff was very hard for me. The other dancers were very glad to be back. I wasn't. I had felt much more relaxed, much more myself during the layoffs. That was another clue to my changing focus.

The ballet world is very tight and restricted. I was raised in an atmosphere that had many other interests, and for me drawing was always an important one. Drawing had always come easily to me, whereas ballet had not, and because the drawing was easy, I never saw it as work. I'm a person who likes to overcome obstacles. I had to be a ballet dancer, but I was not a naturally-built ballet dancer. I really had to work like hell, fanatically!

All of these things started to work on me, and during the last year in the company I was very unhappy. I stayed only because there was a big tour of Europe coming up and my brother, then a musician and now a fine painter, convinced me that if I left then I'd regret it. Once I had tasted Europe, that was it! I just felt that I was finished with the professional dance world, and when I walked away from it I knew I'd never go back. When I finally went to Balanchine to say I was leaving, he was very nice. All he said to me was, 'Well, we all have to find our own roads in life and I wish you luck.' Many others said, 'Don't worry. You'll be back. You won't know what else to do. You'll miss it. You'll want to teach.' I have gone back many, many times to watch, and I have never once regretted leaving. I have never once wanted to go back to a class. (I've never stopped working out, however. I still do one hour each morning — a combination of jazz, modern, ballet, and yoga. I cannot imagine letting my body turn into pudding!) From the day I left, I have felt absolutely free. Of course, after you leave there are all the difficulties that come up in life. In my case there were financial difficulties, and the problems of starting a new life abroad. Nevertheless, I've been much happier and have felt much more fulfilled since I left the ballet.

I lived in Paris for a while, where I foolishly tried to become a fashion model. Another life of looking skinny and trying to be beautiful! (Though as a result I met some wonderful people, including a fashion photographer and an editor for *Vogue*.) They saw some work I had done as an illustrator and encouraged me to keep up with that aspect of my life. They also saw *The Dancing Witch*, a book that I wrote and illustrated during my last year with the company. At that time, I showed it to one of the other dancers who was married to an editor at McGraw-Hill. She took it to him and his company published it in 1965.

I've now had six children's books published. I continue with the books, but to a lesser and lesser degree. My goal is to be a painter which is the ultimate expression for me, though it must be noted that the art world is as competitive, if not more so, than the dance world.

I lived in Majorca, off and on, for twelve years. I spent many years in a wonderful mountain village called Deyá but, like the ballet, the atmosphere there became very close. Everyone knew everyone else, and it got too tight and too stale, beautiful as it was. I'm a person who gets restless and who needs new environments. I try to live in Europe for several months each year. For a long time that was more fulfilling for me. Now I feel equally at ease in the States. I do feel more at home professionally in New York. Ideally, I'd like to live in Europe some months of every year, prepare new work and bring it back to the States to show and sell.

More recently, I've been living in Paros, Greece, for half the year, in an old country house up in the hills. The life there is primitive, but it's what I want: living simply with time to paint. I paint all day in a relaxed atmosphere. I'm there to produce work so that I can either come back to New York to sell it or have something ready for the future. There are local galleries, so I've started exhibiting my work in

Greece and that is something new for me.

I'm constantly working, whether I'm in Greece, in central Europe, or in New York. That's a remnant of my ballet training — discipline. However, I've found that I can't make much money in Europe. I explored the possibilities in England and France, but I can earn two or three times as much in America. I suppose I'm accustomed to the very tight, highly paced level in New York, too.

I would like to have good returns on my children's books because I put so much work into them. I work very hard. This is also true in my personal life. Nothing comes easily. I want certain things and I never compromise. I could never settle for a husband and children because it was the time for that, or because it was the thing to do, or because of my insecurity. I'm not interested in that form of security. My security is my family background, travel, and work. I would like a strong relationship and/or a child, but those things would have to be shaped to my lifestyle. I've seen that done by my friends who live in Majorca and travel about the world. On those terms I would want it very much. I would want a man who was understanding of my needs, my freedom, and my creative intensity. But that's been very difficult to find because, although many men say they understand, they don't really when it comes down to it, and you're left alone again. In Europe I have a network of very good friends who are important to me. I know I can depend on them and, if I'm on my own, they are always there.

This style of living may sound romantic, and in many ways it is. You get to live in beautiful places, but it's difficult and it's lonely. You are not in a family structure as you are in the ballet and financially it's a struggle. While the loneliness is hard to deal with, that's part of it, part of the independence and the sense of being free. Many people try to put you into a structure and you have to struggle constantly to hold on to your independence.

Aloneness is very necessary for me and I love it. I love solitude. But loneliness is something that creeps up on you, and you begin to wonder, 'Is it worth it? This is my work in front of me. Is it really good enough?' I've applied very high standards to everything I've done. I feel fortunate to have worked with Balanchine, to have known Hofmann, and to have been published. They all had very high standards of professionalism. I'm used to that now and I like it.

Now I'm trying to break into the art world and my standards remain very high. That's one of the reasons my life is a constant struggle. It's mostly hard work, with very few rewards and a lot of rejections. With the children's books, I got so used to rejections that I used to laugh. I got to the point where rejection slips were my old friends (though a couple of times I was ready to throw it in — but I couldn't). It was worth everything if you got a call from one of the big publishers who wanted to do your book, because then you knew, deep down inside of you, that you had a well-founded belief in your own talent. I think that part of the satisfaction of being an artist is acceptance by the public. I think it's fine to paint in your studio by yourself. It's fine to have great ideas about what you want to do. But then you have to go out into the competitive world, and that is one of the challenges that I like in life.

Another area in which I have worked is the production of educational film strips. It turned out to be wonderful training because you have to work fast, you have to work to a deadline, and you have to be very technical. I never went to art school so I had to learn film-strip technique while I was working. It brought me into contact with the commercial world. I also enjoy freelance illustrating. It's nice money and good practice. I hired an agent and from time to time she has found work for me. One of these jobs was illustrating someone else's book. I had always had a horror of that, but once I did it, it was fine. In the long run, any art work you do will keep your technique going. When my own book characters are accepted, or my paintings, it's a wonderful feeling. Then it's my family and my children that are accepted.

In 1982 I participated in a huge exhibition of children's book art, and for the first time I was surrounded by other illustrators of children's books. I looked at them and I felt a great comradeship, a great love for all of them, because I knew exactly what they were going through. They were all hard-working, dedicated illustrators. Rather than having a sense of competition, I felt very open and good about them and their work. I had the same feeling when I participated in my first group show in a New York gallery. And now, looking back, I feel absolutely the same way about dancers."

# ARLENE SHULER

*"I think a career in dance can enrich what you do after performing and make it fuller. If I had to do it all over again, I would do it exactly the same way. I'm glad I was a dancer. It's shaped my life, it's shaped my vision, and I think it's made me better at what I do."*

*Photograph by Pamela Craig with permission from the National Law Journal*

Arlene was born in Cleveland, Ohio, and took her first ballet classes there. When she was thirteen, her family moved to New York and she continued her dance studies at the School of American Ballet. During her first year there she was chosen to dance the role of Clara in The Nutcracker with the New York City Ballet. In 1965 Arlene auditioned successfully for the Joffrey Ballet and was accepted as an apprentice, dancing regularly with the company and later becoming a full company member and soloist. She danced with the Joffrey Ballet for four years and decided to leave in order to re-evaluate what she wanted to do.

After working for a year as an advertising and demonstrator co-ordinator with a cosmetics company and having developed an interest in politics, Arlene enrolled in the School of General Studies at Columbia University and completed her degree, majoring in political science. Even though a scholarship student, she had to work part-time as a typist to support herself throughout her college years. Upon graduating she was accepted into Columbia Law School.

After her first year at law school, Arlene was awarded an internship at the National Endowment for the Arts in Washington, D.C., and managed to maintain her contacts with that organization throughout her law studies by doing some consulting work. On completion of her law studies, she became Program Administrator of the Dance Program at the NEA. After passing her final bar exam, she worked for New York Congressman Ted Weiss in Washington for two years, developing arts legislation. She then moved back to New York and accepted a job as Executive Director of Volunteer Lawyers for the Arts, where she worked until recently. Arlene is now Deputy Director of the Wallace Funds, a group of foundations established by the founders of Readers' Digest.

"When I was six, my mother took me to dance class in Cleveland, Ohio, where I was born. I was told I was talented, so I continued. Then when I was thirteen, my family moved to New York and I began to study seriously at the School of American Ballet. At first I was in awe of everyone at the school and I found it very competitive. Janet Reed, who was the ballet mistress at the time, invited me to audition for the role of Clara in The Nutcracker and I was chosen to be one of the four Claras that year. Being Clara was one of the most exciting experiences of my life.

My ambition was to get into the New York City Ballet, although I must say that at the time I wasn't that enamoured of some of the more avant-garde Balanchine works. I wanted to be a 'Swan Queen' and to dance in Giselle, but there didn't seem to be that many other alternatives. When you're at the School of American Ballet, that's all there is

186

— especially in those days. I also went to the Professional Children's School. (I did the whole thing!) Unfortunately, it became clear in a couple of years that I was not a Balanchine dancer. I was short (in the days when he didn't take short dancers) and didn't have a perfect body or the kind of strong technique he required. A lot of dancers in my class did get into the company, but I didn't. Of course I was devastated. The day I didn't get into the special class Balanchine had formed for the most promising students was heartbreaking.

I was, however, very good academically. I was the top person in my class, so there was always the alternative of going to college. When I was about sixteen, I got a severe case of mononucleosis and hepatitis and was out for three months over a summer, and during that time I took an in-depth look at what was happening. I was very discouraged and didn't know what to do. When you're at the School of American Ballet, there's nothing else filling your thoughts but the possibility of dancing with the New York City Ballet. I was faced with whether or not to go to college, but around that time, 1965, the Joffrey company began to reorganize. I auditioned, and Joffrey was interested and took me into the company as an apprentice.

In those days there wasn't a second Joffrey company, so the apprentices rehearsed and danced with the company off and on. It was a full schedule because I was there through the last half of my senior year in high school. At the same time I was focusing on my ballet technique, because School of American Ballet training is based on a perfect body and if you don't have a perfect body you do things incorrectly. Mr. Joffrey, who is an extraordinary teacher, helped me and that really made a big difference.

After a while I got into the company, but it took me a long time because I had so much to re-learn. It wasn't an easy experience. I was insecure. Even though I felt I was good enough to get into the company, I only knew that I was very unhappy. Of course, there were some great moments. Eventually I did the lead in Kurt Jooss' *The Green Table*, which was important to me and very fulfilling. When there was a really good, new work, it was exciting, and I loved being on tour — we didn't do that many one-night stands so there was some really interesting touring.

Around this time I started going out with someone who wasn't in the dance world, and for the first time I was exposed to other things, and that had a big influence on me. One day I was in a rehearsal for a lead role in a ballet I'd both understudied and performed. One of the ballet masters started screaming at me that I hadn't improved and what's wrong with me, which was common. Normally, I would have gone into the dressing room and cried. This time I went into the dressing room and said, 'I'm angry. Why am I taking this?' All of a sudden I realized that I hadn't been happy even in performing, and I said, 'I'm going to quit.' Several months later that's exactly what happened.

It was a particularly bad year at the Joffrey. One of the dancers had committed suicide (although it had nothing to do with the company). He was a very close friend and it had a profound effect on me. About a month later someone else in the company took an overdose of sleeping pills. The worst experience for me at that time concerned another dancer whose fiancé was killed in a fire. She was a close friend and I was to be maid of honor at their wedding. It made me realize how quickly time goes by. She had spent so little time with him because of dancing, and then he was dead. When all these things happened, they reaffirmed my decision to leave. I had begun to realize how ephemeral our lives as dancers were. I say to people now, I missed the sixties — they passed me by. At the time I understood that there was something else out there, but I didn't really know what it was.

I realize now that it was much harder to quit than it would have been to go on dancing with the company because I was giving up a very secure 'family.' Being in a ballet company is very womb-like, very close. Everyone really takes care of one another despite the competition. To leave it for this really vast unknown was frightening. My friends were all in the company, and I didn't know what I was going to do. I thought of going elsewhere, but it seemed like failing to leave New York.

When I told Joffrey I was leaving, he didn't seem terribly surprised and in fact was very supportive. For the next six months (which is how long my unemployment insurance benefits lasted), I did nothing. I was going out with a man and I started seeing him more, cooking dinner and being domestic. I read a little and collected unemployment. I didn't go to museums or study anything, and I didn't even miss dancing. That shocks me to this day! I didn't go back to ballet classes or even go to see a performance for a year. I don't even remember feeling depressed. It was strange, however, that I could just cut out something that I had done almost every day of my life for fifteen years; and I didn't feel the need to do any other exercise. Looking back, I must have been in quite a deep state of depression.

After a year I did go to see a performance of the Joffrey company. They did *The Green Table*, which was one of my favorite pieces, and *Trinity*, which really looked like fun to dance. I had just broken up with my boyfriend and I went because I thought I might dance again and go back to my dance family. I went backstage to the dressing room at City Center, and everyone was sitting in the same places and doing the same things. They had remained part of the continuum of ballet company existence, just as I had for all those years, and I knew that now I was somehow different. They hadn't changed at all. I had changed a great deal and knew then that I couldn't go back. The sadness was that I lost my friends when I left. Even though I would occasionally see people afterwards, we no longer had anything in common. Eventually, the friendships tapered off.

When unemployment ran out, I got my first job. I had taught myself how to type on my father's thirty-five-year-old manual type-writer, and I went for a job interview. It was at a cosmetics company. I did their typing test and my result was minus ten, because I was so slow and had so many mistakes. They hired me anyhow as an advertising and demonstrator co-ordinator because they loved the idea of having an ex-Joffrey ballet dancer on staff. Every job I've had since then has always been, in part, because I was an ex-Joffrey dancer. To this day people introduce me and say, 'This is Arlene Shuler. She's a lawyer and was a dancer at the Joffrey Ballet.' It used to bother me because it seemed as if I had no identity except as an ex-dancer, but now it's actually very helpful, so I don't really mind.

In that first job, since I really couldn't type and they realized I was pretty smart, I got my own little department. I stayed there for a year. It was very interesting and very commercial — the high-tech business world! By the time the company went bankrupt in 1970 I had become interested in politics, mainly by following newspaper reports of the Cambodian situation. I went to work for a congressman thinking that would be one way of learning about politics. It was really interesting for a while. Then I had a couple of other jobs and finally, during the second year, I realized that I needed to go to college. It took me two and a half years from the time I stopped dancing to actually enter college.

I thought at the time that I wanted to work in government. When I went to Columbia University's School of General Studies (which is for people who are a little older), I majored in political science.

During the whole time I was in college, I had to work part-time doing typing to make enough money to support myself. I got scholarships for school, and with additional loans I could pay my tuition, but I couldn't live. By then I had become a good typist. I soon realized, however, that I needed a professional degree, because I didn't want to have to continue to type for someone else for a living.

Getting a master's degree in something was not insurance enough, so I considered going to law school. The alternative degree seemed to be in public administration and was offered by the Woodrow Wilson School at Princeton. The decision was made easy for me when I got into law school a year early at Columbia. There was an accelerated program there, and two people from each division were taken after only three years of undergraduate work. I did very well in college, and well enough on my law board entrance exam to get into that program. It made law very attractive. Even though I felt I needed this degree, I didn't enjoy law school at all. I only wanted the piece of paper that was going to make sure I got the kind of job I wanted.

The fact is, I have never practiced. After my first year in law school someone told me about an internship program at the National Endowment for the Arts. I applied and got an internship through Kathleen Bannon. She, of course, loved the fact that I had been a dancer and was now in law school. There aren't too many professional ballet dancers who are in law school or are lawyers. (Delia Peters of the New York City Ballet is now at Columbia Law School, and Helen Heineman of the Harkness Ballet graduated from Yale Law School in 1984.) I went to the Planning Office of the Endowment, and while I was there I realized that I could actually work in the arts. I could be an arts administrator, and I could combine my education and training with working in the arts. This was a revelation! I had not known about the National Endowment for the Arts when I was dancing, but once there I loved it.

I was offered an opportunity to stay at the Endowment before I graduated from law school. It was very tempting, but I decided to return to school. During that second year I continued to work at the Endowment as a consultant, and I did a position paper for the Planning Office. I flew back and forth frequently and was able to maintain my contacts there.

After my second year I worked for a law firm for the summer, because I thought I should give it a try. I didn't like it very much even though the practice specialized in arts and entertainment law. Then it

190

turned out that there was an opening at the dance program of the National Endowment. It was offered to me and I went to Washington and became the Program Administrator, which was the number two position. I was commuting, taking courses in New York, and at the appropriate time I took the exams and finished my law degree.

I worked in the dance program for a little over a year and then did some other consulting at the Endowment in a different area. I wanted to move back to New York and thought I had another job there, but the job fell through at the last minute. So there I was in Washington not knowing what to do. I decided to take the bar exam, which I had never taken, and passed it, which was very nice. Then I got a job working for Congressman Ted Weiss. I spent two years working for him in Washington, developing arts legislation and holding hearings on the National Endowment for the Arts. It was a very interesting experience, but I still wanted to move back to New York.

A job opened up at Volunteer Lawyers for the Arts, a nonprofit organization which provided free legal services for needy artists. They were looking for a lawyer with arts experience and funding backgound, and there I was with the perfect requirements. I knew several people on the board, and they hired me as Executive Director. I worked there for four years and it was a fantastic job that brought together all my interests, including helping small dance companies and choreographers.

Now I have a wonderful new job as Deputy Director of the Wallace Funds. I'm also Chairman of the Board of Directors of David Gordon's dance company. I'm involved with a lot of people in the arts and I don't do any legal work, which suits me quite well. I would rather take my training and the background and credentials that being a lawyer gives me and use them for other purposes. It has been worth every hour and every penny of going to law school and becoming a lawyer for the advantages I have in the professional world. Getting a job as an executive director of a relatively important service organization after working only three years couldn't have happened without that degree.

I think that I developed some sense of purpose in my life, especially after I went to the Endowment, and realized that I could work in the arts. That experience was pivotal. Most of my friends are involved in the arts, and I now have a much broader knowledge of the whole arts and dance community. When I spoke in 1984 at the Dance USA Conference, there were many people there with whom I'd been involved along the way in dance, and so getting back there was really a terrific experience. I think a career in dance can enrich what you do after performing and make it fuller. If I had to do it all over again, I would do it exactly the same way. I'm glad I was a dancer. It's shaped my life, it's shaped my vision, and I think it's made me better at what I do."

# ROLAND VAZQUEZ

*"At first I missed all the lights and the applause. I felt I had trained and performed all that time and all of a sudden it was over. I was sort of an outcast and it bothered me for a while. But that time was very, very short."*

*Photograph by Martha Swope*

*Photograph by Delia Peters*

*Roland was born in Oakland, California, and took his first dance classes there, studying Spanish dance, tap, and ballet. He continued his dance studies throughout his academic schooling. After he finished school, he was drafted into the army for two years. On his release, he decided to resume his dance training and studied with the Christensen brothers at the San Francisco Ballet. He was taken into the company and became a soloist and a principal dancer. He danced with the company until early 1951 when he decided to go to New York.*

*In New York, Roland first joined the Slavenska-Franklin Company, dancing and touring with them for a few seasons before joining the Metropolitan Opera Ballet. While still at the Met, he successfully auditioned for Balanchine, and he joined the New York City Ballet in 1955. He danced with the company for fourteen years, eventually becoming a soloist.*

*Roland was offered the job of assistant stage manager at the New York City Ballet, and even before he stopped dancing had combined working backstage with performing. Since his retirement from performing, he has worked as stage manager for the New York City Ballet. Roland is married to former dancer Viola Crucil and they have two children, Yolanda Marie and Roland, Jr.*

"I was born in Oakland, California, and took my first dance classes there. My sister was a flamenco dancer, and I think I must have been about seven when I started studying Spanish, tap, and ballet. Throughout my school days I continued with these dance studies, but at that stage I wasn't too impressed with the profession. My mother wanted the two of us to be dancers. She came from Mexico and wasn't allowed to be involved in theatre. It was not the custom of her family and she could not be involved in show business. Theatre was taboo. She wanted me to do something that she couldn't do. I got a lot of flack from my schoolmates about my dance classes, which is why I hated it. I couldn't stand it because you weren't one of the 'regular' people. You were an eccentric, an oddball.

After I finished school I was drafted and spent two years in the service. On my release I had the 'G.I. Bill,' but I didn't know what to do with it. My mother asked me if I would attempt the theatre again. I said yes, because it would enable me to meet a lot of people. Ordinarily I was sort of a loner and the theatre was very educational for me. Once I got started I did meet a lot of people, fantastic people. I felt it was all wine, women, song, and parties, and I thought, 'Well, that's what I want to get into!'

I went to the San Francisco Ballet and studied with Harold and

William Christensen and then with Lew Christensen. I think they gave me a lot of good basic work and all three of them were very different. If you wanted to be a big star (which I never achieved, by the way), you had to put your full concentration on your work. I accomplished quite a bit in the short time that I studied with the Christensens.

I was taken into the San Francisco Ballet and that was the start of my career. After a while, I became a soloist and then a principal dancer with the company. I think it was by pure accident! I happened to be there at the right time. I stayed until early 1951. At that time there was not much going on as far as performances were concerned. There was only the opera season, which was two to three weeks in San Francisco and two weeks in Los Angeles. It wasn't quite enough work to sustain the body, and they only paid you when you performed. It wasn't too healthy and you had to look for other work, so I came to New York.

I was out of work for ... it couldn't have been more than three weeks! I ran into Alexandra Danilova at the School of American Ballet, and she happened to need a partner for the Slavenska-Franklin Company. I was fortunate enough to be hired. I danced with them for a few seasons and it was quite an experience. I was not used to performing continuously under difficult touring conditions. Two years of one-night stands and traveling by bus is not really very glamorous. There was often no linoleum on the floors. There were even warped floors, holes in the floors, and nails sticking up. We toured mainly in the States, but we did go to Japan for about three or four weeks and then to Manila. That was the extent of our touring abroad. There were six or seven women in the company, including Mia Slavenska and Alexandra Danilova and about five men, including Frederic Franklin. We performed small ballets: cut versions of *The Nutcracker, Coppelia*, and *Swan Lake*. The company was successful everywhere we performed. We went to many little towns in the U.S. and to Canada as well, performing in Vancouver, Victoria, and Montreal.

These days you are not going to see the same things — there is a progression in dance — it's like building a new car every year. Last year's model is not as good as this year's model — and next year's model is going to be better than this year's! Today, the corps de ballet dances more strenuously and exactingly than they used to twenty years ago. On the other hand, in those days the dancers had a lot of qualities that we don't see now.

It was fortunate that while I was with the Slavenska Company I had worked with Zachary Solov, who was Ballet Master at the Metropolitan Opera Company, when he created a ballet for Danilova. I auditioned for him and got into the Metropolitan Opera Ballet. There, I danced with Alicia Markova and I did *Carmen* with Janet Collins. In 1955, while I was still with the Met, I auditioned for Mr. Balanchine with Marian Horosko and both of us were accepted into the New York City Ballet. I loved working with Balanchine. He was very simple to work with, easy, the nicest person. There are no words to describe him. I danced with the company for about fourteen years and I eventually became a soloist. I stopped dancing when I was in my forties, and in the last few years of my dancing career I was actually doing two jobs.

I had been dancing a long time, and I was fortunate to be offered the position of assistant stage manager for the company. I didn't know anything about it at first, but I learned easily enough. The assistant stage manager had left and they needed someone to replace him, so they thought I might be interested. I accepted the job, which at first didn't conflict with the dancing, but I ended up doing the two jobs at once. In a situation like that you learn fast. It's difficult, though, if you're dancing on stage and things have to be done offstage and you are responsible. There are times when you simply can't be in two places at once! Towards the end of my performing career it became a conflict, and I felt the time had come to retire gracefully from dancing.

At first I missed all the lights and the applause. I felt I had trained and performed all that time and all of a sudden it was over. I was sort of an outcast and it bothered me for a while. But that time was very, very short. I was married by then to Viola Crucil, with whom I had danced some principal roles at the Met. Almost two years after we were married we had our first child — a girl, Yolanda Marie — and then a year later, we had our son Roland, Jr. My daughter is now twenty-four and my son is twenty-two, and neither of them wanted to be in the theatre as they grew up.

When I retired from dancing I took a cut in pay. But it wasn't so bad, because you learn to sort of exist on what you make. It was fortunate that I wasn't changing professions in the sense of leaving the theatre, and I already had the other job. When I stopped, I stopped completely and I've never taken class since. I miss that now, and I think everybody should keep exercising because it's advantageous to their bodies. My wife has stopped dancing professionally for some twenty years, but she has never stopped exercising. Every day, six days a week, she works out for forty-five minutes. She puts her tights and toe-shoes on and she works on her own. I don't have that kind of drive. But she says it's a 'must' for her.

I love my work here at the New York State Theater. I know this theatre intimately. I danced here and it's a beautiful place. You have all the conveniences, everything: a nice floor, lots of space, and all the best technical equipment. The company waited a long time for this and eventually they got it. I was part of that and I'm proud of that fact. Basically I'm very comfortable now and I'm happy. I've been with the company for over thirty years and I don't even have my gold watch yet! I've done very well with them and they've been very, very pleasant and wonderful to me. I have no complaints. Whatever happens from here on is another story. I believe in fate — what is meant to be, will be. Our experiences are so personal and unique that it's difficult to know just what would be of help when I'm asked to give advice to dancers. People don't like to take advice, they like to find things out for themselves, and they should!"

# WILLIAM WESLOW

*"I thought I would die when I was asked to leave the company. It happened out of the blue, and I had no earlier thought that I was ever going to stop dancing. I thought that I'd go right into character parts and maybe coach the dancers."*

*Photograph by Martha Swope*

*Photograph by Kenn Duncan*

*Bill started studying dance with Mary Ann Wells in Seattle, Washington, when he was nine and continued to train with her until he left school and joined the U.S. Coast Guard. He spent two years stationed in Alaska, and upon his release from the service he returned to Seattle and resumed his training with Miss Wells. After six months he went to New York and studied with Anatole Vilzak and Ludmilla Schollar.*

*In New York, Bill successfully auditioned for the Broadway show* Annie Get Your Gun *and became lead dancer after a year. In 1949, he joined American Ballet Theatre for a year and a half and then returned to the Broadway stage to appear in the musical* Call Me Madam. *Later, he rejoined American Ballet Theatre for their tour of South America. Following that tour he worked as a soloist in television and at Radio City Music Hall. He then auditioned for the New York City Ballet and was accepted into the company, joining them for their 1958 tour of Japan and Australia. Bill danced with the company for fourteen years, becoming a soloist.*

*On leaving the company he developed a professional massage practice and has become known as a "masseur to the stars," as many prominent entertainment personalities, including Dick Cavett, Billie Jean King and Lee Radziwill form the base of his clientele.*

"I started studying dance in Seattle when I was nine. I had lost my mother when I was five and I was kind of a wild kid who loved to hunt and fish. A friend of the family had told my father that if anybody could handle Bill and give him some sort of future, it was Mary Ann Wells who taught ballet there. I was taken to her school and Miss Wells said, 'If he's talented, I'll keep him, but if he's not I won't bother, because there are too many other students that need my help.' I went every day for about an hour and she worked with me. She said, 'He hasn't much turn-out, or good feet, but he has quality and I think he'll be a very good dancer if he wants to work.' I was given a scholarship. Miss Wells was an extraordinary woman with unorthodox but effective ways of teaching. She was a great teacher and among her other pupils were Robert Joffrey and Gerald Arpino. In addition to ballet, she used to make us study ballroom, modern, and Spanish dancing.

I studied with Miss Wells until I went into the service during the war. I joined the Coast Guard when I was eighteen and was stationed in Alaska. At that time I still had no thoughts of being a professional dancer. I thought I'd like to be a forest ranger. However, when I got out of the service I went back to study with Mary Ann Wells for six months. She suggested that I go to New York. I did, and I studied with

204

Anatole Vilzak and Ludmilla Schollar on the 'G.I. Bill of Rights.' Vilzak liked me very much because I had a good technique and I could turn well. After a while I auditioned (through Duncan Noble) for Helen Tamiris at the Imperial Theatre, and was given a part in *Annie Get Your Gun*. I understudied Daniel Nagrin, whom I eventually replaced as leading dancer. The 'star' was Ethel Merman — a great gal! By this time I had decided I wanted to dance, but I had it in the back of my mind that I really wanted to be in ballet. That's what I'd studied all my life and I loved being in ballet more than anything else. It gave me so much satisfaction because I could do so many different roles. In musicals you do the same part over and over, and it can become very boring.

From *Annie Get Your Gun*, I went to American Ballet Theatre in 1949. I did get some solo roles, thanks to John Kriza, but I got discouraged after a while because there were problems involving jealousy over roles among several of the leading dancers. I was with Ballet Theatre for a year and a half, then I left and went back to Broadway and another musical, *Call Me Madam*, again with Ethel Merman. I had been in that show about six months when Lucia Chase called and said that American Ballet Theatre was going on a tour of South America and, since I knew all the repertoire, would I go? I said, 'Fine,' gave my notice, left *Call Me Madam*, and went to South America.

When I returned, I worked for a while in television and at Radio City Music Hall, and then I decided to audition for the New York City Ballet. I was accepted just before the company's Japanese-Australian Tour of 1958. The tour was one of the great highlights of my life, and I loved Japan very much. I stayed with the New York City Ballet for fourteen years. I especially loved the New York City Center. It had a smaller stage than the New York State Theater, but it was wonderful and very warm. I loved the intimate dressing-rooms and the feel of the stage. When the company moved to the New York State Theater, it bothered me. I missed the small theatre and the warmth from the audience. I never felt the same warmth in the New York State Theater — but perhaps that was just me. A lot of the other dancers, I'm sure, do love it.

When I first joined the New York City Ballet in 1958, it was a smaller company than it is now. We had sixty to sixty-five members and we had to dance many different roles. Everyone got along well and we all knew each other. Later it was completely different. As far as I'm concerned, ballet is becoming much more commercial. The companies are larger and dancers are turned out like hotcakes from the large schools. There are many more dancers and fewer good ballets. We don't have the choreographers that we did then. We had wonderful choreographers like Balanchine, De Mille, and Tudor. As for the dancers, I find them less dedicated now. I think the differences I see have a lot to do with the fact that dancers in the past were brought up in an old-fashioned way, with strict discipline in ballet class, and that dancers just loved to dance — for the joy of it not just for the money.

Teaching, too, has changed. The great teachers made you aware of this great power going through them and through you. They made you dance, made you turn out, and made you do those wonderful steps. They used their hands to make you more aware. Teachers don't touch dancers today. Balanchine always did. We danced differently because of those extraordinary teachers. I think it's very important for students to be able to look to the teacher for help. A student can come into class very depressed and ignore the teacher. The teacher should realize this and might put an arm around him and say, 'Fine, I know you don't feel well, but we're going to do a good class. You'll soon feel much better. Come and talk to me after the class.' This has to do with being aware of what's happening with students. It has to be personal!

While I was in the New York City Ballet I discovered that I had a natural gift for massage. I started out by massaging fellow company members like Eddie Villella. Later, if he did a concert and I could get away, I'd go with him and massage him. After I had left the company and was working as a masseur, he would take me along on these tours. We became the greatest of friends.

I never thought about the end of my dancing. I had always thought my career would go on in the company. I was very happy, and although I was getting older and couldn't jump as high as the younger dancers, I loved it and everything that went with it. It was my life. I had hoped to go into character parts and maybe coach the dancers. This was an area where Balanchine was so very important. He would work with you and tell you the little things that you weren't doing, or things that you might do better. Often you didn't realize that a step could look like that. He would inspire you to do something different with a step. It was Balanchine, the master teacher, wanting you to do something in a unique way. I thought I would die when I was asked to leave the company. It happened out of the blue, and I had no earlier thought that I was ever going to stop dancing. I thought that I'd go right into character parts and maybe coach the dancers.

I think now that dancers in companies should prepare themselves for the day when they will not be able to dance any longer. It's really incumbent upon the manager of a company to get the dancers thinking about what they will do after they dance, especially when they're getting older and their prowess as a dancer is lessening. Normally they will just go on without thinking about their future because what they're doing at the time is occupying all their thoughts and taking all their energy.

I had a terrible time just after I left the company. I went into a depression and I never took another class. If you're out of sight, you're out of mind with dancers, and I wasn't around the theatre all the time. They just forgot about me. I was alone in my apartment ready to kill myself because I was so depressed about not dancing, not hearing music, not being around the theatre and the dancers I so loved working with. It was really devastating to me and I did think about taking my life.

Eventually, however, I decided to take up massaging professionally. I had been doing it for some dancers all along, and Eddie Villella still had me work on him regularly. I went to school and learned all the necessary stuff. While I had some clients besides those from the ballet, it was really Dick Cavett who most helped me get established by referring important people to me.

Now I'm known as a 'masseur to the stars.' I also have policemen, firemen, and construction workers that I love to massage because they're so different from theatre people. They're more down-to-earth and actually more gracious, and they have a great sense of humor too. The famous take it for granted that you can do something for them.

It's been fourteen years now since I stopped dancing, and the anger I felt at the time of my dismissal has lessened. I've committed myself to being a masseur and I enjoy the people that I have as clients. I have some wonderful new celebrities that I massage and it's very beneficial to me. However, I always miss dancing and I sometimes wonder if any dancer ever feels fulfilled. I would really love to coach and teach. I'm doing less in the way of exercise now, although I do work out twice a week, through Billie Jean King's generosity, at a wonderful institute in New York. I would like to do more, although as you get older it's harder. I think more exercise and possibly teaching and coaching, as well as my massaging, would be a wonderful combination.

I hope that in the future so much may not be expected of a dancer in terms of sacrifice. I think they will be paid very well and will have better working conditions, although conditions were not so bad for us when you consider that we worked under someone like Balanchine. In the future, you won't have a Balanchine. Dancers will have to find their own motivation. I've always loved to just get out there and dance. I've gone from the Broadway stage to ballet and television, and back to ballet. What I loved most of all was joining the New York City Ballet, where I fulfilled my ambition to dance many kinds of roles. That's why it was so difficult for me to leave. I loved being in the company, and it was very difficult, ending my career on a comparatively sour note, but now I have another life. The thing that keeps me going is meeting and helping new people. I have to be a masseur, psychiatrist, and confidant all rolled into one.

Looking back on my career, I'd never have done anything the same. People tried to guide me years ago and I simply wouldn't listen. Dancers are very difficult to guide. I would have joined the New York City Ballet long before I actually did. I would have tried to save some money and tried to focus on what I was going to do after I stopped dancing. I can see a certain progression in dance now, and I'm happy that ballet is being accepted all over the world. Personally, I would like to just go on with my work and be a success. Of course, I'd also like to make some money and buy a piece of property (something that I've never been able to do until now). I'd like to have a garden and just enjoy the simple life, probably in Alaska, because I've been fishing and hunting there every season for the last six years. When I come back, I've gained weight; I've eaten a lot of fresh fish and breathed that wonderful Alaska air. It primes me for the year to come. It's a good life!"

# VALERIE WILDER

*"Many dancers seem to feel that dancing takes such focus and concentration that the minute they start thinking of their next career they are in danger of dissipating that concentration and not dancing as well as they might. It's as if the admission that there is something else in life would alone be enough to undermine their performance!"*

Photograph by Joe Myers

*Photograph by David Street*

*The daughter of American missionaries, Valerie grew up in Japan and began her ballet studies there at age seven. At fifteen she was accepted at the Royal Ballet School in London, England, and studied there for two years. She then returned home to Japan for a year and, while completing her high school studies, continued her dance training there. Following that year she came to North America, passing back through London so as to attend a three-month summer training program at the Royal Ballet School.*

*In the United States, Valerie decided to study at Butler University, where she attended for two years. While at Butler she joined a university-based, touring ballet company. A visiting teacher encouraged her to travel to Toronto and study at the National Ballet School with a view to eventually join the National Ballet of Canada. In the course of studying at the ballet school, she became an apprentice with the company and in that capacity joined their tour of Japan in 1970. Upon returning from that tour, she was accepted into the company, dancing with them for over eight years.*

*During her second year with the company Valerie was elected by the dancers to be their Equity representative and the following year was part of the contract negotiating team representing the dancers. Assisted by courses she took at the University of Toronto, Valerie developed as a financial consultant to the dancers, and by the time she decided to stop dancing had already laid the groundwork for a successful new business venture offering financial and contractual counselling services for dancers and other performing artists.*

*Valerie represented the late Erik Bruhn in many of his engagements, including the initial contract negotiations for the Artistic Directorship of the National Ballet of Canada. She was invited by him to join his artistic management team as Artistic Administrator of the company, a position he created for her. Since Erik Bruhn's death, Valerie, along with Lynn Wallis, is now an Associate Artistic Director of the National Ballet of Canada. She is married to Geoffrey Perry, and they have two children, Stuart and Sabina.*

"I grew up in Japan, and when I was about four I went to see the *Takarazuka Theatre*, which is a well-known all-female revue in the city of that same name in southern Japan. The program changes each month, and I happened to go when part of the performance was a ballet. I decided at four that that was what I wanted to do. Living in Japan made it difficult to find lessons, and my parents didn't take me too seriously. At seven I was still agitating to begin ballet classes and so they enrolled me in a local school, where I started taking lessons once a week. I quickly realized that I needed more. I tried various things and even wrote away to the Bolshoi at one point, asking if I could go there.

Eventually, at fifteen, I was accepted at the Royal Ballet School in London. I left Japan, went to London, and studied there for two years. It was a very exciting time to be there, as Nureyev had just defected and was dancing with Fonteyn at Covent Garden. The company didn't have the rehearsal studios close to Covent Garden then, so both the company and the school were all under one roof, and you got a real sense of what the company was doing and what professional ballet was all about. Physically, it was hard for me, because my previous technical training hadn't been very good, and so to train every day under that kind of pressure and be far away from home was difficult. I was more prepared mentally because I had read just about every book and magazine on dance there was to be had in Japan. Also, since Japan was often visited by companies touring abroad, during the time I lived there I was exposed to practically every major ballet and contemporary company, and I continued to see as much as I could in London.

I went to the Royal Ballet Upper School with the expectation of continuing academic studies along with, naturally, intensive ballet training. Although most students didn't go this route, the school brochure had stated that academic studies were available if one wanted them. The reality was that one or two people met about once a week to half-heartedly work on their 'A' levels (final high school grades in England). Midway through the year even this feeble effort ceased and I was quite disappointed. If my parents had known they were sending me off halfway through high school with no real chance of pursuing academics, I'm sure they would have had second thoughts. Although I continued to read a great deal, I concluded that I didn't really want to go through the rest of my life without even a high school diploma, especially if I ended up living in North America.

So after two years in London, I went home to Japan and completed my last two years of high school in one year by taking two courses of everything and studying every day, including Christmas, for the whole year. It was quite a load of work.

I went to a school there called Canadian Academy, which is a school for children of foreign diplomats, business people, and missionaries living in Japan. Because the school was founded by Canadian missionaries and followed the Ontario system of education, one graduated with an Ontario-accredited diploma. One could even do

Grade 13 there. My parents are Americans and were in Japan because they were missionaries. Oddly enough, they ended up serving for a number of years under the Board of Overseas Missions of the United Church of Canada. As a student at Canadian Academy I was starting each day singing 'God Save the Queen' and 'O Canada.' Since a lot of my friends were Canadian too, it was quite natural for me to eventually come to Canada.

After that year in Japan finishing up high school, I came to North America. En route I did pass back through London, however, and took an intensive three-month ballet course there over the summer. I needed to get back into shape because, although I had taken lessons throughout that year in Japan, it had not been very consistent.

At this point my mother strongly suggested that I pursue some university education. Because I'd been in London in the professional ballet environment, I knew that if I did that I would be jeopardizing my chances of ever dancing in a company. Eventually I acquiesced and went to Butler University in Indianapolis for two years.

Two things happened there. First, the university had a little company of about twenty dancers that toured around the Midwest. It was fun, it was good experience, and I got to do some fairly nice roles. The other thing that happened was that I really excelled in academics. One term I got straight A's, and it was very satisfying to me. I found I enjoyed studying, especially sciences, and I was quite flattered to have several department heads try to get me into their areas. However, at the same time, Margaret Saul was teaching ballet at Butler, and she encouraged me to try to join the National Ballet of Canada. I came to Toronto after the first year at Butler, and Betty Oliphant agreed that I had a good chance of getting into the company.

After completing my second year at Butler I came to study full-time at the National Ballet School, including intensive apprenticing with the company. I was with the company throughout the period that Peter Wright was teaching *Giselle*, and then, later that summer, I went to Japan with the company as an apprentice. I joined the company as a full-fledged member right after the Japanese tour and danced with them for eight years. In a sense I feel it was just over nine years because I spent most of that previous period with the company.

I think I always had a very realistic attitude about what I wanted. Right from the first ballet that I ever saw, I wanted to be a very good corps de ballet dancer. That was my ambition and that's what I did. I wanted to dance a lot, and, of course, in the corps one is always 'on.'

Because I was quick and could learn fast, I found myself being used a great deal in all kinds of ballets. If one is not trying to fight for roles or a promotion, then being in the corps de ballet can be very satisfying. In retrospect, my professional dance career was very happy. The choice of joining a major company and being in the corps rather than going to a smaller company and perhaps going further was a conscious decision. Growing up in Japan, where to be part of a group is very much the thing to do, influenced my thinking. Before I went to Canadian Academy I went to Japanese kindergarten and primary school, so I definitely was influenced by this group spirit (shudan ishiki).

While I was dancing I never really got out of academics. When I first came to Toronto I was partly apprenticing and partly at the school, and I took a couple of courses at the University of Toronto. When I joined the company I did stop academics for two or three years, but I soon resumed taking one course at a time, then two at a time.

Much to my surprise — I think it was my second year in the company — I was elected by the dancers to be their Equity Deputy (representative for the union, Canadian Actors' Equity Association). The following year was one of our 'every-three-year' contract negotiation periods, and I was elected to be on the negotiating team. This involved doing some financial projections which were instrumental in changing the whole payroll structure for the dancers. Basically, my calculations highlighted the fact that certain categories of dancers weren't getting the same salary advancement as others. In fact, the longer one stayed with the company, the worse the salary increases became!

It was a tough negotiating session, taking arbitration and another year or so before it was finally settled and the dancers very nearly went on strike. I thought to myself, 'Well, here I am representing sixty-five dancers, and I'm up against lawyers and businessmen who really know what they're talking about.' And I thought, 'Well, I should at least know a little something about all this if I'm going to continue to represent the dancers.' As a result, I started taking courses in accounting, business, and economics.

I believe (and I find it true even now when I'm with the company in a different capacity) if you can focus on something else, there is a lot of time to prepare for another career while one is still performing. There's time between rehearsals, unexpected breaks, travel time, and

215

time in hotel rooms in the morning before class. It takes discipline and the ability to concentrate, blanking out the conversation and casual chitchat, and switching one's focus very quickly from dancing full-out to studying full-out.

My life has always been varied. By the time I was doing my university courses and ballet, I was married to someone who was completely out of the dance world. In fact, he was working at one of the big accounting firms as a management consultant. We met in New York when I was at Butler University and he was at the University of North Carolina. I visited his campus a couple of times and we were both quite serious about ourselves academically. I can't remember a time when I was absorbed only in dance. Even at the Royal Ballet School I gravitated towards a group of students who, although studying dance full-time, were very interested in reading and studying. None of this little group ended up being professional dancers for any length of time. One is now a doctor, another is a designer/writer, and so on. Somehow I always had another side to me, and I'm not sure exactly why that is.

By the time I began to think about leaving the company, I had completed a number of courses, and also had many business contacts in accounting, legal and professional service areas. One thing lead to another, and I became the person whom the dancers turned to for everything from balancing cheque books to advice on whether or not to buy a car — a sort of unofficial general financial adviser. In 1976, two years before I stopped dancing, I went one step further by trying to teach some of the dancers how to do their own income tax returns. My husband and I had little seminars in our home. We both thought that dancers needed to have something put away for that almost inevitable break between a professional dance career and the start of a new career. Dancers usually retire well before sixty-five and often need a re-training period, and we were trying to help put together savings plans and various budgeting systems to prepare them for that hurdle.

The response was fairly good, but really, in the end, what it boiled down to was that most of the dancers wanted someone who could do all that for them. They didn't really want to do it themselves. I started, for a small fee, doing income tax returns and helping them put budgets together. By this time, more and more people were coming to me for various types of advice, and I was still dancing. It was getting to be almost more than I could manage, and my husband and I were thinking of having children. I wasn't sure that I really wanted children, but I had a feeling that if I did have a child, and enjoyed it, I would probably want to stay home.

I made the decision to stop dancing at the beginning of a season, in effect deciding to dance one more year. My little business was thriving and I had a whole year to cope with doing both. I also had a recurring bad hip that season. By the time the year was up, I was really ready to stop. Now I think I almost danced one year too long, but I guess one year too long is better than one year too short!

As soon as I stopped, I took a two-month trip home to Japan and visited old friends and then came back to Canada and started my business full-time. I soon became pregnant and had Stuart that year. Three years later I had another child, Sabina. By the time the second child came along my business was really thriving. It had become obvious that there was a need for this kind of general financial and contractual advice for dancers and other performing artists. While I had gathered a fair amount of knowledge through my work with artists and the courses which I continued to take at university, I was not a chartered accountant and was not fully professionally qualified. Whenever I ran into a problem that required legal help or accounting expertise beyond what I was able to give, I had a referral system where certain professionals were my consultants. When an artist received an offer of a guesting job, I would often negotiate the terms and sometimes actually write up the contract and I found that to be a very interesting area. Inevitably, the business got bigger and more difficult to handle. I kept hiring various people to help me through some of the clerical work. Just before the birth of Sabina, I began thinking that maybe I should cut down and make the business much smaller. I wanted to continue the contract negotiations, budgeting, and financial counselling, but considered eliminating the straight income-tax work.

I first met Erik Bruhn when we were both dancing in the company, and I began to work for him in the taxation and contract negotiation areas while I was still performing. I had been working closely with him for almost six years when, in August of 1982, we got together for one of our normal meetings. Among other things that day I briefed him on the status of the National Ballet's search for a new Artistic Director. Once again, Erik had been approached for the job and this time he was seriously considering it. As he was to be out of the country for several months, I agreed to act as his negotiator with the

National Ballet's Board of Directors to see if an agreement could be reached.

Right at the onset, Erik's demand was that at least one person join him in a capacity that he, at that time, referred to as co-director. He wanted somebody who could work with him very closely in an artistic and administrative capacity. Erik had previously been the artistic director of the Royal Swedish Ballet and knew exactly what running a ballet company involved. He had retired from a brilliant and all-consuming dance career to become a skilled and intuitive manager, and he didn't want to be in a position where he was in meetings all day long and never got into the studio to work with the dancers. Erik asked me to be that person and, in hindsight, it seems that those transitional years of my business, and working with him professionally, laid the groundwork for what was to follow. I could never have expected that this wonderful opportunity of helping Erik run a ballet company would evolve in the way that it did.

In considering whether or not I would be able to take on the job (especially with a brand new baby at home), foremost in my mind was a belief that the company needed Erik as the director. Having had the good fortune of working with him in several capacities, I knew that the two of us got along well. We rarely disagreed when it came to artistic matters and seemed to come to the same conclusions naturally and easily. Erik thought that the 'chemistry' of our different personalities would be good for the company and I agreed. I decided to throw caution to the winds, liquidate my business, hire a full-time nanny, and rejoin the National Ballet of Canada. My husband was very encouraging as well. He had supported me during all those years of touring and dancing, and he supported me in this next endeavor. But I think it has been harder than either one of us expected. The hours have been excessive, and the family has really had to pitch in and help make this job happen.

The first year at the company was rewarding, but also more difficult than either Erik or I could have imagined. We took it on as a three-year project and, from a performance point of view, the dancers started showing a real excitement and vitality almost immediately, and certainly much sooner than we had anticipated. But, of course, a ballet company is a complex organism and what takes place on the stage is not the end of the story. There were some significant changes to be accomplished throughout the organization, and much of it involved a lot of heartache. In the process a number of my contemporaries, dancers and staff, ended up moving on to new careers.

In our second year we were fortunuate enough to persuade Lynn Wallis, at that time Deputy Principal of the Royal Ballet School, to join us in an artistic management team of three. This set-up had been Erik's preferred structure all along and the positive benefits were felt almost immediately. Perhaps because of our ties as old Royal Ballet School alumnae, Lynn and I developed a very close and enjoyable working rapport. It may have been Erik's insight into the unusual strength of our working relationship which led him to recommend, in the final weeks before his sudden and tragic death, that Lynn and I carry the company forward. As Associate Directors of the company during this difficult period immediately following the loss of Erik, Lynn and I are just now fully appreciating how privileged we were to have been guided by a mentor of such stature and understanding.

The decision to leave a performing career is never an easy one. Many dancers seem to feel that dancing takes such focus and concentration that the minute they start thinking of their next career they are in danger of dissipating that concentration and not dancing as well as they might. It's as if the admission that there is something else in life would alone be enough to undermine their performance! This should be the case in the first few years of a professional dance career when total concentration is required because of the many roles to learn, not to mention the adjustments of fitting into a company environment. But I do think that there comes a point at some stage of a long career where it doesn't hurt to at least look towards the future. To put one's head in the sand and be afraid even to look is very, very dangerous. There's a great deal of time spent just sitting around and chatting, which is valuable and fun, but some of that time can be spent in career planning. A good place to start is by identifying interests, since trying to do something that one doesn't enjoy is counterproductive. Then there are the realities of the job market. For the dancer interested in interior design, there are certain steps which must be taken to prepare for such a career. Even being conscious of the basic requirements of the next job, I think, is a step in the right direction. Without a doubt, if I had not taken university courses while I was a dancer, I would not have been able to either start my own business or be in my present position.

I'm also aware that there are many emotional, sensitive, and gifted dancers who need special understanding when they stop performing. I was fortunate that my first non-dancing job and my present position came to exist, in a way, because I've been able to relate to performing artists. I'm logical, but I'm also very sympathetic because I was a dancer myself. I think that receiving some sort of counselling is probably the only way for some dancers to even look at other areas of employment.

Ballet is a short career; so most dancers are going to have to do something else after they dance. There are various ways to prepare for this even if one doesn't want to think about employment options until the end of the career. One aspect of this is the financial planning which I actively encouraged through my business. In Canada, for example, there are Registered Retirement Savings Plans. Although designed for people who retire at sixty-five and live happily ever after, these plans can be very useful for someone who just needs to take two years off in the middle of a working life in order to make a transition. That kind of budgeting realism can be very useful. The average dancer re-trains and gets going on a new career with at least twenty years of working life left. That's a long time not to be planning for. People don't realize that when dancers retire they may not even have the qualifications for job entry as a bank teller or a general secretary; so it's essential that they get help and guidance, and be aware that some measure of success and fulfillment is possible outside of dance."

# conclusion

When research began for this book in 1983, the only existing scheme to help dancers in transition was the excellent Dancers Resettlement Fund in England. Now, four years later, others exist and some are in formation. The realization that dancers are a valuable resource in society and that the tragedies have been more numerous than the successes has finally captured wide attention. This book has been so long in preparation for precisely that reason. Although this author has been committed to the idea of writing it for some time, it seemed more urgent to establish a Dancer Transition Centre than to publish the book. Research turned up suicides, addictions, breakdowns, and dancers who, quite simply, had vanished. The time had obviously come for action.

The Dancers Resettlement Fund provided an excellent example. Founded in 1973 in Great Britain, and administered by Margaret Lawford (herself an ex-dancer and holder of a degree in vocational guidance), the Fund came into being largely at the instigation of Peter Williams, who is well known for his work with and for the welfare of dancers, as well as for his dance writing. He made the existence of a fund one of the principal recommendations of the ballet section of the Arts Council's Opera and Ballet Report (1966-1969), but it was not until April 1, 1973, that the Resettlement Fund was established under a Trust Deed for "the furtherance and assistance of dancers, so that they may usefully undertake some occupation other than or additional to that of dancer." The Fund operates currently in conjunction with a pension scheme. The dancers contribute 5% of their salaries entirely for the pension, which the companies match by 6.5%, while putting in an additional 10% per dancer for the Resettlement Fund. Thus the fund is supported entirely by the companies. The grant applications are submitted to and approved by the Trustees (two from the Arts Council, two from Equity, one representative from each board of member companies, and three independents). Grants are given for tuition and/or apprenticeship costs, costs of materials involved in the retraining process, and living expenses when necessary. The average grant is for £7,500 and can last up to two years. Many dancers have been retrained in a variety of professions and the acceptance of, and respect for, the Fund as an integral part of dance in England is unquestioned.

In Canada, the Canada Council has commissioned two reports. The first, in 1976, was by Nicole Debrouck and outlined the existing programs for dancer retraining. Although there were several grants for which dancers could apply, there was nothing directly relating to re-training and no central agency where they could get information. Ms. Debrouck's report strongly suggested that such a place should exist. The second report, in 1982, was by Kenny Pearl (now Artistic Director of the Toronto Dance Theatre), and detailed the successful transition history of many dancers, but also outlined the need for a central agency which would deal with the issue. Also in 1982, the Hébert-Applebaum Report, commissioned by the Department of Communications, stated: "The federal government should assist dancers and other artists who have short professional careers to resettle into allied professions where their artistic skills can best be put to use. All the relevant agencies and departments — such as the Department of Employment and Immigration — should be involved and the Department of Communications should assume the leadership role."

As a result of this proven need, and provoked by the results of research for this book, the author initiated action to establish a Dancer Transition Project in December of 1984.

The Dancer Transition Project, co-sponsored by the Canadian Association of Professional Dance Organizations and the Dance in Canada Association (Canada's two national dance service organizations), and funded by the Department of Communications, the Canada Council, the Ontario Arts Council, and the Laidlaw Foundation, was a nine-month plan to research and implement a center to help retiring dancers. A national survey polled 258 dancers. Twenty-three professional companies and several independent dancers were queried as to their perceptions of career change, lifestyle, desire for and thoughts on a transition center, and willingness to contribute on a membership basis. The results showed a clear mandate for the center and the dancers' interest in participating. As a result, the Dancer Transition Centre opened officially on September 1, 1985.

Its programs include personal counselling with psychiatrists, psychologists, and social workers, career counselling with career counsellors, and financial, legal, and academic counselling. Grants are available for retraining and subsistence while doing so, as are grants for courses in skills which may be used in a variety of professions, such as computer usage, word processing, and typing, while the dancer is still performing. Performing dancers may also receive grants for courses which will eventually help in a chosen second career. The Centre has a career resource library, publishes a quarterly newsletter, holds seminars and conferences, and operates as a resource center. Its main office is in Toronto, with regional representation in Edmonton, Montreal, Ottawa, Vancouver, and Winnipeg. The Centre is funded primarily by the "Innovations" program of the Canada Employment and Immigration Commission, which has pledged $500,000 over the first three years, and by the Canada Council, the Ministry of Citizenship and Culture, the Ontario Arts Council, and the Bronfman, Laidlaw, and McLean Foundations. It has a Board of Directors, with Karen Kain, the Canadian ballerina, as its President. Only 18 months old, the Centre has seen a significant percentage of the Canadian dance population.

New York also now has a center. Established in October of 1985, Career Transition for Dancers is sponsored by the Actors' Fund of America. Inspired by a conference at Lincoln Center in June 1982, it was spearheaded by Edward Weston, a former dancer who is now Western Regional Director of the Actors' Equity Association. The purpose of the conference was to "recognize the trauma facing professional dancers at the end of their careers and begin to consider ways and means of assisting them into other professions which can utilize their unique backgrounds and skills." Many distinguished speakers, including Margaret Lawford, reported on the subject, and a resolution was made at the conclusion endorsing the "speedy implementation of a model program which might parallel the Dancers Resettlement Fund of Great Britain to begin the process of assisting dancers through a career transition," and to proceed with fundraising and creating a structure for a model program. The result is Career Transition for Dancers. Diane Nichols, a professional social worker, was the first director and assessed the needs of the dancer and made appropriate referrals. She has now been succeeded by Diane Goldsmith. Financial awards and internships with organizations both within and outside the dance world are available. The organization is currently operating as a one-year pilot program in New York and has been funded for a total of $100,000 by Actors' Equity Foundation, the Screen Actors' Guild, the American Federation of Television and Radio Artists, and the American Guild of Musical Artists. Additional funding was pledged by the Actors' Fund from proceeds from the premiere showing of the movie *A Chorus Line* on December 9, 1985.

From the beginning, Edward Weston envisioned that the model program, serving primarily a New York population, would be expanded to national scope to assist dancers throughout the United States. The plan is for the Actors' Fund to open branches in its facilities in Chicago and Los Angeles.

Career counsellor Ellen Wallach, who has done workshops for the Boston Ballet, the San Francisco Ballet, and other companies, has received grants from the National Endowment for the Arts, the Dayton Hudson Foundation, and the New York City Department of Cultural Affairs to research careers retired dancers have chosen. Her research project, *Life After Performing*, is concluded and the data should prove valuable in many ways.

Another career counsellor, Paula Jaye, has held workshops for dancers in transition in New York and will continue these in the future.

There has been other activity in New York as well. A practical and successful effort has been the counselling work done within the psychiatric component of the Performing Arts Center for Health in New York, an all-encompassing health-care facility expressly created for performing artists. Established in 1981 by Marian Horosko, a former member of the New York City Ballet and currently the Associate Editor of *Dance Magazine*, and Dr. Judith Kupersmith, who also danced with the New York City Ballet and is now a psychiatrist, PACH began seeing dancers in 1982 after a survey of New York's professional dancers had detailed their health care needs and concerns. Dancers were seen by Dr. Kupersmith, the psychiatric head of PACH, and her staff and are sometimes referred to Letitia Chamberlain, head of career counselling at New York University. Dr. Kupersmith who recently moved to Louisville, Kentucky, will open a PACH office there at the medical services department of the University of Louisville.

Recently at the San Francisco Ballet, Tim Duncan, Russell Murphy, and Victoria Morgan have initiated many efforts in the area of career transition for dancers. They have helped secure an extensive benefits package for the dancers, including a tax shelter annuity program, and dental and major medical coverage. They have also explored career counselling, by co-operating with San Francisco State College in developing a plan for scholarship availability and use of the college library. Seminars led by Ellen Wallach have been held, and they are working within the community to establish internships in fields dancers have identified as being of interest. To date, they are the first company in the United States to provide such extensive and realistic solutions to the career transition problem.

Obviously the matter is being dealt with on a practical and understanding basis. Those who for so long have subsidized their art with integrity and commitment now have somewhere to turn and be helped. It is only the beginning, but at least it is reality.

Those dancers who have had to do it alone and have succeeded so well — including the dancers interviewed for this book — are an example and an inspiration. We can only imagine the benefits to society now that centers and caring people have extended their help.